STUDY GUIDE

A Raisin in the Sun

Lorraine Hansberry

WITH CONNECTIONS

HOLT, RINEHART AND WINSTON
Harcourt Brace & Company
Austin • New York • Orlando • Atlanta • San Francisco • Boston • Dallas • Toronto • London

Staff Credits

Associate Director: Kathleen Daniel

Managing Editor: Richard Sime

Editor: Catherine Goodridge

Writer: Diane B. Engel

Editorial Staff: *Copyediting Supervision,* Steven Fechter, Abigail Winograd; *Copyediting/Proofreading,* Julie Brye, Susan Kent Cakars, Dorothy Coe, Ed Cohen, Christine de Lignières, Sacha Frey, John Haffner Layden, Lanie Lee, Michael Zakhar; *Support,* David Smith, Kristin Wodarski; *Word Processing Supervision,* Laurie Muir; *Word Processing,* John Falcon, Louise Fernandez

Editorial Staff: Jason Tougaw, Abigail Winograd, Laurie Muir, Steven Fechter

Permissions: Mark Hughs, Lee Noble

Design: Betty Mintz

Production/Manufacturing: Athena Blackorby

Photo Research: Mary Monaco

Production: Carol Marunas

Front cover: foreground image of Sidney Poitier and Ruby Dee by Photofest.
Background wrap image: houses on the south side of Chicago, April 1, 1941.
Hulton Getty/Liaison Agency.

Printed in the United States of America

ISBN 0-03-055107-2

3456 085 02

TABLE of CONTENTS

FOR THE TEACHER

FOR THE STUDENT

Using This Study Guide

Approaching the Play

The successful study of a play often depends on students' enthusiasm, curiosity, and openness. The ideas in **Introducing the Play** will help you create such a climate for your class. Background information in **About the Writer** and **About the Play** can also be used to pique students' interest.

Reading and Responding to the Play

Making Meanings questions are designed for both individual response and group or class discussion. They range from personal response to high-level critical thinking.

Reading Strategies worksheets contain graphic organizers. They help students explore techniques that enhance both comprehension and literary analysis. Many worksheets are appropriate for more than one set of scenes.

Play Notes provide high-interest information relating to historical, cultural, literary, and other elements of the play. The **Investigate** questions and **Reader's Log** ideas guide students to further research and consideration.

Choices suggest a wide variety of activities for exploring different aspects of the play, either individually or collaboratively. The results may be included in a portfolio or used as springboards for larger projects.

Glossary and Vocabulary (1) clarifies allusions and other references and (2) provides definitions students may refer to as they read. The **Vocabulary Worksheets** activities are based on the Vocabulary Words.

Reader's Log, Double-Entry Journal, and **Group Discussion Log** model formats and spark ideas for responding to the play. These pages are designed to be a resource for independent reading as well.

Responding to the Play as a Whole

The following features provide options for culminating activities that can be used in whole-class, small-group, or independent-study situations.

Play Review provides a format for summarizing and integrating the major literary elements.

Play Projects suggest multiple options for culminating activities. **Writing About the Play, Cross-Curricular Connections,** and **Multimedia and Internet Connections** propose project options that extend the text into other genres, content areas, and environments.

Responding to the Connections

Making Meanings questions in **Exploring the Connections** facilitate discussion of the additional readings in the HRW LIBRARY edition of this play.

This Study Guide is intended to

- ***provide maximum versatility and flexibility***
- ***serve as a ready resource for background information on both the author and the play***
- ***act as a catalyst for discussion, analysis, interpretation, activities, and further research***
- ***provide reproducible masters that can be used for either individual or collaborative work, including discussions and projects***
- ***provide multiple options for evaluating students' progress through the play and the Connections***

Literary Elements

- plot structure
- major themes
- characterization
- setting
- point of view
- symbolism, irony, and other elements appropriate to the title

Making Meanings Reproducible Masters

- First Thoughts
- Shaping Interpretations
- Connecting with the Text
- Extending the Text
- Challenging the Text

A **Reading Check** focuses on review and comprehension.

The Worksheets Reproducible Masters

- Reading Strategies Worksheets
- Literary Elements Worksheets
- Vocabulary Worksheets

Reaching All Students

Because the questions and activities in this Study Guide are in the form of reproducible masters, labels indicating the targeted types of learners have been omitted.

Most classrooms include students from a variety of backgrounds and with a range of learning styles. The questions and activities in this Study Guide have been developed to meet diverse student interests, abilities, and learning styles. Of course, students are full of surprises, and a question or activity that is challenging to an advanced student can also be handled successfully by students who are less proficient readers. The interest level, flexibility, and variety of these questions and activities make them appropriate for a range of students.

Struggling Readers and Students with Limited English Proficiency: The **Making Meanings** questions, the **Choices** activities, and the **Reading Strategies** worksheets all provide opportunities for students to check their understanding of the text and to review their reading. The **Play Projects** ideas are designed for a range of student abilities and learning styles. Both questions and activities motivate and encourage students to make connections to their own interests and experiences. The **Vocabulary Worksheets** can be used to facilitate language acquisition. **Dialogue Journals,** with you the teacher or with more advanced students as respondents, can be especially helpful to these students.

Advanced Students: The writing opportunity suggested with the **Making Meanings** questions and the additional research suggestions in **Play Notes** should offer a challenge to these students. The **Choices** and **Play Projects** activities can be taken to advanced levels. **Dialogue Journals** allow advanced students to act as mentors or to engage each other intellectually.

Auditory Learners: A range of suggestions in this Study Guide targets students who respond particularly well to auditory stimuli: making and listening to audiotapes and engaging in class discussion, role-playing, debate, oral reading, and oral presentation. See **Making Meanings** questions, **Choices,** and **Play Projects** options (especially **Cross-Curricular Connections** and **Multimedia and Internet Connections**).

Visual/Spatial Learners: Students are guided to create visual representations of text scenes and concepts and to analyze films or videos in **Choices** and in **Play Projects.** The **Reading Strategies** and **Literary Elements Worksheets** utilize graphic organizers as a way to both assimilate and express information.

Tactile/Kinesthetic Learners: The numerous interactive, hands-on, and problem-solving projects are designed to encourage the involvement of students motivated by action and movement. The projects also provide an opportunity for **interpersonal learners** to connect with others through play-related tasks. The **Group Discussion Log** will help students track the significant points of their interactions.

Verbal Learners: For students who naturally connect to the written and spoken word, the **Reader's Logs** and **Dialogue Journals** will have particular appeal. This Study Guide offers numerous writing opportunities: See **Making Meanings, Choices, Play Notes,** and **Writing About the Play** in **Play Projects.** These options should also be attractive to **intrapersonal learners.**

Assessment Options

Perhaps the most important goal of assessment is to provide feedback on the effectiveness of instructional strategies. As you monitor the degree to which your students understand and engage with the play, you will naturally adjust the frequency and ratio of class to small-group and verbal to nonverbal activities, as well as the extent to which direct teaching of reading strategies, literary elements, or vocabulary is appropriate to your students' needs.

If you are in an environment where **portfolios** contain only carefully chosen samples of students' writing, you may want to introduce a second, "working," portfolio and negotiate grades with students after examining all or selected items from this portfolio.

The features in this Study Guide are designed to facilitate a variety of assessment techniques.

Reader's Logs and Double-Entry Journals can be briefly reviewed and responded to (students may wish to indicate entries they would prefer to keep private).The logs and journals are an excellent measure of students' engagement with and understanding of the play.

Group Discussion Log entries provide students with an opportunity for self-evaluation of their participation in both play discussions and project planning.

Making Meanings questions allow you to observe and evaluate a range of student responses. Those who have difficulty with literal and interpretive questions may respond more completely to **Connecting** and **Extending.** The **Writing Opportunity** provides you with the option of ongoing assessment: You can provide feedback to students' brief written responses to these prompts as they progress through the play.

Reading Strategies Worksheets, Play Review, and Literary Elements Worksheets lend themselves well to both quick assessment and students' self-evaluation. They can be completed collaboratively and the results shared with the class, or students can compare their individual responses in a small-group environment.

Choices activities and writing prompts offer all students the chance to successfully complete an activity, either individually or collaboratively, and share the results with the class. These items are ideal for peer evaluation and can help prepare students for presenting and evaluating larger projects at the completion of the play unit.

Vocabulary Worksheets can be used as diagnostic tools or as part of a concluding test.

Play Projects evaluations might be based on the degree of understanding of the play demonstrated by the project. Students' presentations of their projects should be taken into account, and both self-evaluation and peer evaluation can enter into the overall assessment.

The **Test** is a traditional assessment tool in three parts: objective items, short-answer questions, and essay questions.

Questions for Self-Evaluation and Goal Setting

- What are the three most important things I learned in my work with this play?
- How will I follow up so that I remember them?
- What was the most difficult part of working with this play?
- How did I deal with the difficulty, and what would I do differently?
- What two goals will I work toward in my reading, writing, group, and other work?
- What steps will I take to achieve those goals?

Items for a "Working" Portfolio

- reading records
- drafts of written work and project plans
- audio- and videotapes of presentations
- notes on discussions
- reminders of cooperative projects, such as planning and discussion notes
- artwork
- objects and mementos connected with themes and topics in the play
- other evidence of engagement with the play

For help with establishing and maintaining portfolio assessment, examine the **Portfolio Management System** *in* **ELEMENTS OF LITERATURE.**

Answer Key

The Answer Key at the back of this guide is not intended to be definitive or to set up a right-wrong dichotomy. In questions that involve interpretation, however, students' responses should be defended by citations from the text.

About the Writer

Lorraine Hansberry

A brief biography of Hansberry appears in* A Raisin in the Sun, *HRW Library edition. You may wish to share this additional biographical information with your students.

Lorraine Hansberry (1930–1965) was the youngest of four children. Her parents were prominent intellectuals, and in their South Side Chicago home, Hansberry met some of the greatest African Americans of their generation, including the poet Langston Hughes, the musician-composer Duke Ellington, the athletes Joe Louis and Jesse Owens, the actor-singer-activist Paul Robeson, and the writer-civil-rights leader W.E.B. Du Bois.

Hansberry's parents had experience in politics and activism. In 1938 Carl Hansberry challenged the segregated housing pattern in Chicago when he purchased a house in an all-white neighborhood. The family was threatened by a white mob and forced to leave by a court order. Hansberry took the case to the Supreme Court *(Hansberry v. Lee)* where he won a favorable judgment.

Despite the victory, the experience left him disillusioned and bitter, and these feelings resonate throughout *A Raisin in the Sun,* which Lorraine Hansberry completed in 1957. Her dramatization of one family's struggle to make a place for themselves in an unfair, even hostile world attracted a great deal of attention when it became the first play by an African American woman to be produced on Broadway. The play's première, in 1959, was a cultural event, giving voice to a generation ready to be heard. Hansberry dramatized the dreams and disappointments of African Americans in general, but she also depicted an ordinary family whose struggles, conflicts, and triumphs all people could recognize. *A Raisin in the Sun* won the New York Drama Critics Circle Award that year, a first for any African American playwright. The play crossed social lines with a powerful grace, appealing to critics, activists, and artists, as well as theatergoers.

Although her life and career were cut short by an early death, Lorraine Hansberry left behind an important legacy. Before she turned to drama, she worked on Paul Robeson's progressive magazine, *Freedom,* as a writer and editor. And in addition to *A Raisin in the Sun,* she wrote several other plays, including *The Sign in Sidney Brustein's Window* and *Les Blancs.* Much of her work was collected and arranged in "an informal autobiography" by her ex-husband, Robert Nemiroff. The result, *To Be Young, Gifted and Black,* is a tribute to Hansberry's literary, social, and personal vision.

More on Hansberry

Carter, Steven R. ***Hansberry's Drama: Commitment Amid Complexity.*** Urbana: University of Illinois Press, 1991.

Cheney, Anne. ***Lorraine Hansberry.*** Boston: Twayne Publishers, 1984.

Domina, Lynn. **Understanding A Raisin in the Sun: *A Student Casebook to Issues, Sources, and Historical Documents.*** Westport, Conn.: Greenwood Press, 1998.

Keppel, Ben. ***The Work of Democracy: Ralph Bunche, Kenneth B. Clark, Lorraine Hansberry, and the Cultural Politics of Race.*** Cambridge, Mass.: Harvard University Press, 1995.

Leeson, Richard M. ***Lorraine Hansberry: A Research and Production Sourcebook.*** Westport, Conn.: Greenwood Press, 1997.

Scheader, Catherine. ***Lorraine Hansberry: Playwright and Voice of Justice.*** Springfield, N.J.: Enslow Publishers, 1998.

Sinnott, Susan. ***Lorraine Hansberry: Award-Winning Playwright and Civil Rights Activist.*** Berkeley, Calif.: Conari Press, 1999.

Also by Hansberry

The Sign in Sidney Brustein's Window (1965)

To Be Young, Gifted and Black: Lorraine Hansberry in Her Own Words, adapted by Robert Nemiroff (1970)

Les Blancs: The Collected Last Plays of Lorraine Hansberry (1972)

A Raisin in the Sun: The Unfilmed Original Screenplay (1992)

About the Play

Special Considerations

The major sensitive issue in this play is racial prejudice; it is faced and commented on (with occasional antiwhite epithets) by all the adult Youngers. (Note: The epithet *nigger* is used by Mrs. Johnson, a minor African American character, to refer to other African Americans. She is taken to task by Mama for the usage. The Connection *My Dungeon Shook* by James Baldwin also contains the word *nigger.* The play contains some expletives as well, especially in the "eat your eggs" passage.) Other possibly sensitive issues are Walter Lee's abuse of alcohol and his disparagement of women (particularly his wife and his sister); Ruth's contemplation of an abortion (which she ultimately rejects); and Beneatha's argument against the existence of God.

For Viewing

Lorraine Hansberry: The Black Experience in the Creation of Drama. Princeton, N.J.: Films for the Humanities, 1975. A dramatic blend of material from Hansberry's writings.

A Raisin in the Sun. New York: Columbia Pictures Home Entertainment, 1982. The 1961 film version with performances by Sidney Poitier and Claudia McNeil.

A Raisin in the Sun. Malibu, Calif.: Monterey Home Video, 1996. The 1989 made-for-TV version of the play.

To Be Young, Gifted and Black. Malibu, Calif.: Monterey Home Video, 1996. Film based on the book and the stage play.

For Listening

Lorraine Hansberry Speaks Out: Art and the Black Revolution. New York: Caedmon, 1970, 1972. Interview.

A Raisin in the Sun. New York: Harper Audio, 1991. Reissue of the 1972 Caedmon audiotape. Unabridged reading.

Historical Context

In *To Be Young, Gifted and Black,* Lorraine Hansberry writes of a childhood trip to Tennessee to visit her maternal grandmother. She remembers her mother pointing to the nearby hills and telling Hansberry's brothers that their grandfather had hidden there from his master when he was a little boy. The strength that came to Hansberry from her heritage shines clearly in her play.

Hansberry also had an early fascination with Africa. An uncle, William Leo Hansberry, an authority on African antiquity, encouraged her interest. Hansberry later spent a year studying African history with W. E. B. Du Bois. That interest in Africa is embodied in Joseph Asagai, the character in *A Raisin in the Sun* who encourages the Youngers to learn about their African heritage and to "live the answer" to their problems.

For the Youngers' real-life counterparts, the 1950s was a tumultuous time, one that would change America. With the rise of the civil rights movement, the voices of African Americans who cried out for change swelled. The scholar Margaret B. Wilkerson points out that *A Raisin in the Sun* mirrors its era in a host of ways:

> The newly militant mood of black Americans, born of anger, frustration, and deferred dreams, had been captured in the explosive and desperate Walter Lee. The sudden decision of Rosa Parks, whose refusal to move to the back of a bus precipitated the historic Montgomery bus boycott, was mirrored in Lena Younger's apolitical decision to live in Clybourne Park and her consequent challenge to the restrictive covenants of the day. The rise of independent African nations was reflected in the presence of the African student Asagai, who brought to the play the reality of his people's struggle for liberation; Beneatha's adulation of things Africaine anticipated a new wave of hair and dress styles that black Americans would soon adopt. . . . The play touched the vibrating nerve of a country on the verge of change and a people on the move.

Literary Context

As a child, Hansberry learned to love books, especially works of history and biography. She came to know the writings of Frederick Douglass, the nineteenth-century abolitionist who, after escaping from slavery, was one of the first African Americans to gain a wide readership. Douglass inspired Hansberry by what she called the "breadth of his vision" and the "wedding of intellect to action."

While a freshman at the University of Wisconsin, Hansberry had a career-shaping moment as she watched a campus performance of *Juno and the Paycock* by the Irish playwright Sean O'Casey. *Juno* is a play of strong emotions, with themes relating to the struggle against poverty and the strength to be found in one's heritage—Irish nationalism, in this case. "I remember sitting there stunned with a melody that I thought might have been sung in a different meter," Hansberry later recalled. "I did not think then of *writing* the melody as I knew it—in a different key; but I believe it entered my consciousness and stayed there." She noted that from O'Casey she learned about "the genuine heroism which must naturally emerge when you tell the truth about people. This, to me, is the height of artistic perception and is the most rewarding kind of thing that can happen in drama." Hansberry returned to the campus theater again and again, her appreciation for the power of the stage growing.

Several powerful African Americans influenced Hansberry's work. (Their influence has been noted by several critics; for more information, see the chapter that Anne Cheney devotes to the topic in her critical biography *Lorraine Hansberry.*) One was Paul Robeson, founder of *Freedom* magazine and Hansberry's employer for nearly three years. Robeson's highly visible and often controversial political stance deeply impressed Hansberry. For her, he was "a voice, member and champion of the people's struggle." The political elements of *A Raisin in the Sun* and her other works owe much to him. Similarly, W. E. B. Du Bois, a friend of Hansberry's parents, served as a mentor. Through his example, Hansberry saw the need for African Americans to seek higher education (as does Beneatha in this play) and positions of leadership (as Asagai does, albeit in Africa). Hansberry called Du Bois "an institution in our lives, a bulwark of our culture."

An important literary influence was the writer and long-time Hansberry family friend Langston Hughes. His poems in particular helped Hansberry see the beauty in the expression of African American culture. In fact, the original title of *A Raisin in the Sun* was *The Crystal Stair,* an allusion to Hughes's poem "Mother to Son." Although Hansberry eventually chose a title from a line in "Harlem," another of Hughes's poems, the play still reflects the determination to overcome life's difficulties that is central to "Mother to Son."

Critical Responses

The first major critical reaction to *A Raisin in the Sun* came from Philip Rose, a music publisher and a friend of Hansberry's. Rose was so won over by the play that he and a partner, David J. Cogan, determined to take *Raisin* to Broadway. The journey was not easy: Broadway producers considered the drama too risky or too limited in appeal to be financially successful. Rose and Cogan raised the money themselves and opened the play first in New Haven and then in Philadelphia. Enthusiastic reviews prompted the Schubert organization to offer performance space in Chicago and New York.

When *A Raisin in the Sun* opened on Broadway, on March 11, 1959, critics raved. The play won the New York Drama Critics Circle Award that year and Lorraine Hansberry became the first African American playwright (as well as the youngest person and the fifth woman) to be so honored. The play was a milestone in the careers of the actors who appeared in it, and its popularity inspired other African Americans to become involved in the theater.

Before long, however, negative criticism also surfaced. Because the play was a commercial success and seemed to exemplify the passive-resistance kind of civil rights activity that militant groups disparaged, some critics wondered if its characters were "authentically" black. In response, Hansberry acknowledged,

> "They're trying to say that it isn't a propaganda play, that it isn't something that hits you over the head; they are trying to say that they believe the characters in our play transcend category. . . . I think people, to the extent we accept them and believe them as who they're supposed to be, to that extent they can become everybody. So I would say it is definitely a Negro play before it is anything else."

Years later the writer Amiri Baraka concluded that he and other militants had "missed the essence of the work. . . . What is most telling about our ignorance is that Hansberry's play still remains overwhelmingly popular and evocative of black and white reality, and the masses of black people dug it true."

A Raisin in the Sun has become a classic American play. On the silver anniversary of its première, Frank Rich of *The New York Times* eulogized Lorraine Hansberry as "a compassionate writer who asked her public to reexamine the deferred dreams of black Americans."

The Play at a Glance

Plot and Setting

A Raisin in the Sun is set in Chicago's South Side, in the early 1950s. On stage we see the Youngers' apartment, clean but clearly demonstrating "the living of too many people for too many years." The plot unfolds over a few weeks. It builds on the promise of a brighter future, symbolized by the payout from an insurance policy held by the family's late patriarch. As the Youngers discuss this money, conflicts within the family surface. Conflicts outside the family add to the tension and underscore the state of race relations in the world at large. The climax is a make-or-break moment. The resolution reveals both the strength of the family (and the community the family represents) and the triumph that comes when a person who feels beaten by life rejects the temptation to despair.

A **Play Review** that includes **plot** and **setting** appears on page 37 of this study guide.

Major Characters

Lena Younger (Mama) is a recent widow, and years of hard work are catching up with her. She worries about her family and wrestles with decisions about the insurance money. She dearly wants to give more responsibility to her son. One of the joys at the end of the play comes when he proves himself worthy of her trust.

A **Literary Elements Worksheet** that focuses on **character and characterization** appears on page 38 of this Study Guide.

Walter Lee Younger, Mama's thirty-five-year-old son, works as a chauffeur but dreams of owning his own business. So strong is this dream that he neglects his marriage, drinks to excess, and betrays Mama's trust by treating her money carelessly. His redemption at the play's climax is so powerful because his mistakes have been so devastating.

Ruth Younger is Walter's wife and the mother of their son, **Travis.** She is desperate to see her family in a home of their own. Ruth is torn between her disgust with Walter's present behavior and her love for the man he once was.

Beneatha Younger, Mama's college-age daughter, dreams of becoming a doctor but pursues other interests as well. She is attracted to both **George Murchison,** the son of a wealthy businessman, and **Joseph Asagai,** a politically active student from Nigeria. As her family's conflicts play out, Beneatha must reexamine her own heart.

Themes

The American Dream: The play's epigram asks the question—"What happens to a dream deferred?"—that establishes the major theme. For the most part, the dreams of the major characters have been long deferred, but, ironically, when the chance for fulfillment

Connecting with
ELEMENTS OF LITERATURE

You can use *A Raisin in the Sun* to extend students' exploration of the themes and topics presented in *Elements of Literature.*

- *Third Course:* "The Human Spirit"
- *Fourth Course:* "Dreams—Lost and Found"
- *Fifth Course:* "I, Too, Sing America"

does arrive, their dreams create conflict. As a result, all of the "dreamers" must rethink the nature and the importance of their goals. Ultimately the characters learn that dreams can come true, but that they are precious and rarely come true with ease.

The power of prejudice: Set before the rise of the civil rights movement, *A Raisin in the Sun* reveals a social undercurrent of racial tension. The Youngers know discrimination; in large part it is the reason their dreams have been deferred. Prejudice in an all-white community helps drive the play to its climax, and at the play's resolution the Youngers seem likely to face prejudice again.

From defeat to victory: Years of "doing without" have taken their toll on the Youngers, but the insurance money seems to be the key to victory, the chance to leave the past behind and build a better future. When most of that money is lost, even Mama despairs. Walter, however, causes the family's fall and makes its rebirth possible. His decision not to surrender the house for the sake of its buy-out value provides a moral victory that empowers the entire family.

Conflict

A **Literary Elements Worksheet** that focuses on **external** and **internal conflict** appears on page 39 of this study guide.

Financial issues stir up conflicts in the Younger family, as do such issues as parent-child and male-female relationships and the quest for personal fulfillment. Several of the Youngers are challenged to address internal conflicts and change their own thinking before they can cope with their external conflicts. And at the play's climax, when the Youngers stand together against racial prejudice, many of the family members' own conflicts are settled as they unite in the face of a greater cause.

Motivation

A **Literary Elements Worksheet** that focuses on **motivation** appears on page 40 of this study guide.

One reason Hansberry's characters are so accessible is that their motives, although complex, are clear. The experiences of loss and deprivation are powerful, as are the characters' moral values and self-images. These motives sometimes propel the characters into conflict, but they also enrich the characters and help us to see ourselves in them.

Options

SMALL-GROUP WORK

Financial Planning

Divide the class into small groups, and tell students to think of their groups as families. Each "family" has just won fifty thousand dollars. How will they spend it? Each group member should propose a plan for spending the money. What conflicts arise? How will they resolve these conflicts? Have groups discuss possible solutions and then choose one to share with the class. Later, make connections between this activity and the conflict among the Youngers over their ten thousand dollars.

LIBRARY RESEARCH

Signs of the Times

Tell the class that *A Raisin in the Sun* is set in the early 1950s. Ask students to identify two important events from that decade. One event should relate to American history (such as the end of the Korean War, in 1953) or popular culture; the other should relate to race relations during that period (such as the 1954 Supreme Court ruling that declared the doctrine of "separate but equal" unconstitutional). Have students share their findings (and perhaps use them to create a time line) to give them a feel for the Youngers' world.

AUDIOVISUAL INTRODUCTION

Sounds Onstage

Play at least one audio excerpt of *A Raisin in the Sun.* (See the For Listening suggestions on page 8, or download audio clips from the Internet Town Hall at http://town.hall.org/Archives/radio/IMS/HarperAudio/355_harp_00_ITH.html.) Call on volunteers to give their impressions of the clips and to use the clips as the basis for a few predictions about the play's plot or characters.

READING A SPEECH AND A POEM

Of Dreams and Difficulties

Read or review with students "I Have a Dream," the 1963 speech by Martin Luther King, Jr., which captures the essence of the civil rights movement. Have students list some of the dreams that King mentions. Then, have them read Langston Hughes's "Harlem." Invite comments about the value of dreams and about dreams that are deferred. You might also ask students to suggest which reactions in "Harlem" might result if it were King's dream that was being deferred.

CLASS DISCUSSION

Prejudice

Use students' ideas to develop a semantic web around the word *prejudice.* To stimulate discussion, ask questions such as these: What kinds of prejudices are there? Are any prejudices acceptable? How can you tell that a person is prejudiced? Urge students to keep track of examples of prejudice that they find in *A Raisin in the Sun.*

Plot Synopsis and Literary Elements

Act One

Plot Synopsis

Scene 1: Act One finds the five members of the Younger family crowded into a South Side Chicago apartment that once was a source of pride and hope for Lena Younger (Mama). Over the years the apartment and its furnishings have become shabby, and the family has grown too large for the space.

The action begins on a Friday morning in the early 1950s. Walter Lee Younger, Mama's adult son, disagrees with Ruth, his wife, about giving their son, Travis, money he needs for school. Walter argues with Ruth after Travis leaves, complaining that she does not support his dreams and plans for their future. He also argues with his sister, Beneatha, who refuses to answer his questions about her plan to go to medical school. Clearly Walter resents the fact that he must struggle from one short-lived, low-paying job to the next while Beneatha attends college and may go to medical school as well.

The dialogue reveals that Mama is waiting to receive a check for ten thousand dollars, the benefit from her late husband's life insurance policy. Each adult member of the family has a different plan for the money, a different "dream deferred" that the money can help to fulfill. Thus, a complex set of conflicts develops. Walter wants to invest in a liquor store with his friends Bobo and Willy; Beneatha hopes to go to medical school; Ruth wants a better life for Travis. Mama herself dreams that Beneatha will go to medical school and that the family will move into a two-story house with a yard. In the meantime, though, she must face the squabbling of her "spirited" children. She argues with Beneatha over the girl's ideas about religion. Afterward Mama compares her children to her houseplant "that ain't never had enough sunshine": They all struggle for a better life amid hostile circumstances. As Mama speaks, Ruth faints.

Scene 2: The next morning, Saturday, Mama and Beneatha are cleaning the apartment. Ruth comes home and tells them she is pregnant, news that pleases Mama but disturbs Beneatha and Ruth herself. Next Beneatha receives a visit from Joseph Asagai, a Nigerian student she has been dating. Their discussion quickly becomes political, with Asagai teasing Beneatha about her taking politics too seriously. Underlying their conversation is Beneatha's feeling that her African American heritage is inferior to Asagai's African roots. Mama tries to chat with Asagai about African politics but quickly resorts to a motherly offer of "some decent home-cooked meals." As he departs, Asagai calls Beneatha *Alaiyo,* Yoruba for "One for Whom Bread—Food—Is Not Enough."

The check arrives, and Mama is momentarily lost in thoughts of Big Walter, her husband. Her reverie is broken with Walter's boisterous arrival. When Walter again talks about investing in a liquor store, Mama refuses to listen. She is opposed to the plan. In the argument that follows, Mama points out that freedom is more important than money and that her children have far more freedom than she had. She then shocks Walter with the news that Ruth is pregnant and is ambivalent about the pregnancy. When Walter fails to "stand up and look like [his] daddy"—that is, to go to Ruth and encourage her—Mama calls him "a disgrace to [his] father's memory."

Literary Elements

External and internal conflict: The central **conflicts,** or struggles, among the Youngers are brought to light through the anticipation of the insurance payment, a matter revealed early in Scene 1. As the characters think and talk about the money, they wrestle with their desires but disregard the good of the family as a whole. They also clash with one another and with the constraints placed on them by the state of race relations in the 1950s.

Character and characterization: In Act One, Hansberry introduces several types of **characters:** **flat** (for example, George Murchison) and **round** (for example, Mama), **static** and **dynamic** (as Travis and Walter, respectively, will prove to be), **protagonists** and **antagonists** (in several combinations). The playwright reveals their personalities through their actions, their dialogue (what they say about themselves as well as what others say about them), and the stage directions.

Motivation: The drives that stem from the characters' personality traits, experiences, and values are established early on. Mama, for example, is often motivated by religious convictions and a desire to honor Big Walter's memory; Walter seems to be driven by envy of others' success. Not only does an understanding of motivation help explain the conflicts of the play, but it also enriches appreciation of the characters themselves.

Act Two

Plot Synopsis

Scene 1: That evening, Ruth watches in surprise as Beneatha, dressed in a Nigerian robe that Asagai gave her, begins to dance and sing to a record of Nigerian music. Walter enters. He is intoxicated and is soon swept up in the moment. As he joins Beneatha in the celebration of their heritage, Ruth looks on with amusement and disdain. When George Murchison arrives to take Beneatha to the theater and Beneatha removes the headdress she's been wearing, Ruth is horrified to see that Beneatha has cut off her straightened hair. Beneatha's dismissal of "assimilationist Negroes" prompts George to ridicule her interest in African history and culture. While Beneatha changes her clothes, Walter chats with George. The talk turns ugly when Walter betrays his resentment of Murchison, the wealthy "college boy." After George and Beneatha leave, Walter and Ruth share a rare moment, private and unguarded, as they sadly acknowledge that "something done come down between us."

Mama's entrance ends the conversation. She announces that she has used some of the insurance money to buy a house in Clybourne Park, an all-white community. Ruth is jubilant even though she knows that being the only African American family in the new neighborhood will not be easy. Walter is enraged that Mama has "butchered up" his dream.

Scene 2: On a Friday night a few weeks later, the Youngers are packing. George and Beneatha return from an evening out and argue about the importance of education. After George leaves, Beneatha tells Mama that he is a fool. She appreciates the fact that Mama understands her. At this point, Mrs. Johnson, the Youngers' neighbor, enters. In the guise of a supportive friend, she manages to express her disdain for the "pride" the Youngers are displaying by moving to a white neighborhood. Visibly annoyed, Mama is relieved when Mrs. Johnson finally leaves.

A phone call from Walter's employer reveals that Walter has not been to work in three days. Walter admits that he has spent the time driving, people watching, and visiting his favorite bar. In a tirade he rails against his life and his job. Mama confesses that she has been wrong not to be more supportive of him, and to right the wrong, she gives him $6,500, the remainder of the insurance money after the down payment on the house. She instructs him to set aside $3,000 for Beneatha's education and to take charge of the rest, as "the head of this family from now on." She leaves the room, and Travis enters. Walter embraces his son and promises him a great—but unrealistic—future.

Scene 3: It is a week later, moving day. Walter and Ruth are getting along better. While Mama is out, Karl Lindner, representing the Clybourne Park Improvement Association, comes by. Lindner decries the "incidents" that have occurred after African Americans have moved into "certain areas," and he explains that the residents of Clybourne Park have worked hard to realize their dreams for their community. He then presents the association's offer: They will buy the Youngers' house from them at a profit. Walter shows the man to the door without considering the offer. Later they tell Mama about it and present her with moving-day gifts: gardening tools and a gardening hat.

The mood changes when Bobo arrives. Distraught, he reveals that Willy has absconded with all the money for the liquor-store venture, including the $6,500 that Mama had entrusted to Walter.

Literary Elements

Plot: As Act Two unfolds, the **plot** rises and falls several times as it moves toward a **climax.** The reader might have reason to think that Lindner's visit is the climax of the play and that the Youngers' refusal of his offer provides a resolution, but Hansberry undercuts such expectations with a sudden **reversal**—the loss of the money—signaling that the true climax is yet to come.

Conflict: None of the conflicts established in Act One finds a lasting resolution in Act Two; indeed, tensions increase, and in Scene 3, Hansberry introduces a new conflict: between African Americans and whites in the outside world. That clash affects the Youngers.

Symbol: Several of the objects in Acts One and Two represent abstract concepts that are important in the play. The insurance money is a symbol of the chance to realize dreams, and the new house symbolizes hope. The Nigerian clothes and music represent the family's heritage (from which Walter will draw strength in Act Three). Mama's plant symbolizes endurance despite constricting circumstances, and her gardening tools reflect her nurturing of the lives around her.

Act Three

Plot Synopsis

An hour later the Youngers are still reeling from the devastating news of the lost money. Asagai arrives to encourage Beneatha to "live the answer" to her problems—and to propose that she return to Nigeria with him as his wife. She is unsure, however, and even Mama seems ready to give up her dreams. Walter announces that he has called Lindner and plans to accept his offer. Walter seems resolute even after Mama protests that doing so is a dishonor to their heritage. Even so, when Beneatha says that she despises him, Mama chastises her and urges her to consider the "hills and valleys he come through" before judging him.

Lindner and the movers arrive simultaneously. Mama tells Travis to stay and listen to what his father has to say to Lindner. Walter's respect for himself and his heritage inspires him to reject the offer.

The move begins. Beneatha and Walter leave the apartment, arguing over her plan to marry Asagai and practice medicine in Africa. To Ruth, Mama expresses her pride in Walter. Ruth leaves, and as the stage lights dim, Mama takes a last look around, retrieves her plant, and goes out to greet her future.

Plot Synopsis and Literary Elements *(cont.)*

Literary Elements

Theme: Several themes are reiterated as the play nears its climax and conclusion. Walter's final refusal of Lindner's offer underscores the importance of dreams and demonstrates that when a person stands against prejudice, he or she can turn a seeming defeat into a victory. The outcome of the play also offers several reminders: that strength can come from family ties, that one's heritage is valuable, and that equality and freedom are owed to everyone.

Climax: The play's moment of greatest **tension** and **suspense** results from a devastating turn of events. After they learn that most of the money is lost, the Youngers find that they can stand together despite their differences as they face the future that lies beyond the play's end.

Motivation: All the **motives** established earlier in the play continue to be influential in Act Three. There is an important difference, however: As Walter struggles to claim his self-respect, carrying the family with him, it becomes apparent that people can and will make their own choices about how they will act. This assertion of the independence of the human spirit contributes to the positive message of the play.

Reader's Log: Model

Reading actively

In your reader's log you record your ideas, questions, comments, interpretations, guesses, predictions, reflections, challenges—any responses you have to the plays you are reading.

Keep your reader's log with you while you are reading. You can stop at any time to write. You may want to pause several times during your reading time to capture your thoughts while they are fresh in your mind, or you may want to read without interruption and write when you come to a stopping point such as the end of a scene or the end of the play.

Each entry you make in your reader's log should include the date, the title of the play you are reading, and the pages you have read since your last entry (pages ____ to ____).

Example

Pygmalion

Act One

This play reminds me a lot of another play we read last year: The Importance of Being Earnest by Oscar Wilde. They both seem to be set in a similar time in London, England—the manners and style of some of the characters seem similar. They speak in the same affected kind of tone. Both of the plays are trying to be funny, at least in the beginning, but I think that the characters in Pygmalion are going to be more serious. Some of them are poor. They have accents that are different and the dialogue is more difficult to read. At the end of The Importance of Being Ernest everything worked out in a silly, but neat, way. I don't think that this will happen with Pygmalion.

Exchanging ideas

Exchange reader's logs with a classmate and respond in writing to each other's most recent entries. (Your entries can be about the same play or different ones.) You might ask a question, make a comment, give your own opinion, recommend another play—in other words, discuss anything that's relevant to what you are reading.

Or: Ask your teacher, a family member, or a friend to read your most recent entries and write a reply to you in your reader's log.

Or: With your teacher's guidance, find an online pen pal in another town, state, or country and have a continuing play dialogue by e-mail.

Reader's Log: Starters

When I started reading this play, I thought . . .

I changed my mind about . . . because . . .

My favorite part of the play was . . .

My favorite character was . . . because . . .

I was surprised when . . .

I predict that . . .

I liked the way the writer . . .

I didn't like . . . because . . .

This play reminded me of . . .

I would (wouldn't) recommend this play to a friend because . . .

This play made me feel . . .

This play made me think . . .

This play made me realize . . .

While I was reading I pictured . . . (Draw or write your response.)

The most important thing about this play is . . .

If I were (name of character), I would (wouldn't) have . . .

What happened in this play was very realistic (unrealistic) because . . .

My least favorite character was . . . because . . .

I admire (name of character) for . . .

One thing I've noticed about the author's style is . . .

If I could be any character in this play, I would be . . . because . . .

I agree (disagree) with the writer about . . .

I think the title is a good (strange/misleading) choice because . . .

A better title for this play would be . . . because . . .

In my opinion, the most important word (sentence/paragraph) in this play is . . . because . . .

(Name of character) reminds me of myself because . . .

(Name of character) reminds me of somebody I know because . . .

If I could talk to (name of character), I would say . . .

When I finished this play, I still wondered . . .

This play was similar to (different from) other plays I've read because it . . .

This play was similar to (different from) other plays by this writer because it . . .

I think the main thing the writer was trying to say was . . .

This play was better (worse) than the movie version because . . .

(Event in play) reminded me of (something that happened to me) when . . .

Double-Entry Journal: Models

Responding to the text Draw a line down the middle of a page in your reader's log. On the left side, copy a meaningful passage from the play you're reading—perhaps a bit of dialogue, a description, or a character's thought. (Be sure to note the number of the page you copied it from—you or somebody else may want to find it later.) On the right side, write your response to the quotation. Why did you choose it? Did it puzzle you? confuse you? strike a chord? What does it mean to you?

Example

Quotation	Response
The Note Taker: You see this creature with her kerbstone English: the English that will keep her in the gutter to the end of her days. Well, sir, in three months I could pass that girl off as a duchess. . . . (Act I)	This seems like it might be an important quote in the play. I wasn't sure what the role of the Note Taker was, why he was taking notes and being so rude. Now it seems as if it has something to do with the way the people are speaking in the play. It explains some things but it doesn't explain why he is so nasty.

Creating a dialogue journal Draw a line down the middle of a page in your reader's log. On the left side, comment on the play you're reading—the plot so far, your opinion of the characters, or specifics about the style in which the play is written. On the right side of the page, your teacher or a classmate will provide a response to your comments. Together you create an ongoing dialogue about the play as you are reading it.

Example

Your Comment	Response
The Flower Girl seems a bit silly. She starts to cry and whimper the minute anyone says anything to her and she is always acting on the defensive. I don't see how she and the Note Taker are going to be in the same play.	I don't think that she is silly. She is poor and probably has to worry about the police or having to have a license to sell flowers and she is afraid that the Note Taker is going to do something to harm her. I think that he is the one who is in pain. He is so sarcastic and mean.

Name ______________________________ Date ______________

Group Discussion Log

Group members

____

____

____

____

____

Play discussed

Title: ______________________________

Author: ______________________________

Pages ____ to ____

Three interesting things said by members of the group

____

____

____

____

____

____

____

What we did well today as a group

____

____

____

____

What we could improve

____

____

____

____

Our next discussion will be on ______________________. We will discuss pages ______ to ______.

Glossary and Vocabulary

A Raisin in the Sun

- **Vocabulary Words** are preceded by an asterisk (*). The **Vocabulary Worksheets** draw on these words.
- Words are listed in their order of appearance.
- The definition and the part of speech are based on the way the word is used in the play. For other uses of the word, check a dictionary.
- African words are in italic type.

Act One

***indictment** *n.:* accusation; complaint.

Colonel McCormick: Robert R. McCormick (1880–1955), editor and publisher of the *Chicago Tribune.*

***drily** (also spelled **dryly**) *adv.:* matter-of-factly; without emotion.

***exasperated** *v.* used as *adj.:* irritated; annoyed.

***oppression** *n.:* feeling of being greatly troubled or harshly treated.

ally *n.:* supporter or confederate.

***mutual** *adj.:* shared; held in common.

***anguish** *n.:* pain and suffering; sorrow.

***permeated** *v.:* penetrated and affected every part.

Hereros: a Bantu-speaking ethnic group in Namibia (formerly called South West Africa).

***unobtrusively** *adv.:* without attracting attention; inconspicuously.

***furtively** *adv.:* secretly; stealthily.

***reflective** *adj.:* thoughtful; meditative.

Nigeria: one of the largest and most populous countries on the western coast of Africa. Nigeria was a British dependency when this play opened; it gained independence in 1960.

***raucous** *adj.:* loud; boisterous; rowdy.

Liberia: nation on Africa's west coast, established as a republic in 1847 by formely enslaved African Americans.

Yoruba *adj.:* in the language of the Yoruba, an ethnic group of southwestern Nigeria and parts of Benin and Togo.

assimilationism *n.:* policy of fully absorbing minority groups into the dominant culture so that their members lose their ethnic and cultural identities.

***lynched** *v.:* unlawfully killed by a mob.

Act Two

Butterfly: Madama Butterfly, heroine of the opera of the same name by Giacomo Puccini.

ocomogosiay *interj.:* coined word combining syllables from Yoruba, Swahili, and Zulu to represent a shout of triumph in battle.

Pearl Bailey (1918–1990): American entertainer, singer, and actress. Ruth is imitating her.

alundi: Yoruba for "happy holiday"; here, the first word of a Yoruban harvest-festival song.

Jomo: Jomo (Kikuyu for "flaming spear") Kenyatta, African nationalist leader and first president (1964–1978) of Kenya.

owimoweh *n.:* variation of a Zulu word for "lion."

Chaka (usually spelled **Shaka**) (c. 1787–1828), great Zulu chief and military leader.

Ashanti empires: Reference is to the powerful eighteenth- and nineteenth-century Ashanti Empire in present-day Ghana.

Songhay (also spelled **Songhai**) **civilizations:** Reference is to a fifteenth- and sixteenth-century West African empire and great trading state.

Benin: West African country known for its wooden masks, bronze statuettes, and pottery.

Bantu *n.:* subgroup of languages, including Zulu and Swahili, spoken in central and southern Africa.

***sobriety** *n.:* state of being sober (as opposed to *intoxicated*); clearheadedness.

Glossary and Vocabulary *(cont.)*

Prometheus: in Greek mythology, a Titan who steals fire from the gods and gives it to humans. Zeus, king of the gods, punishes Prometheus by chaining him to a mountain, where each day an eagle eats his liver. Each night Zeus causes the liver to regrow so that the torture is excruciatingly repetitive. Prometheus is finally freed by Zeus's son Hercules.

***resignation** *n.:* passive acceptance; submission.

***revelation** *n.:* disclosure; something made known.

***imploring** *v.* used as *adj.:* pleading.

crackers *n.:* derogatory term for impoverished white people.

***vigor** *n.:* intense strength; vitality.

***exuberant** *adj.:* full of life; uninhibited.

peckerwoods *n.:* derogatory term for impoverished white people.

conked *v.* used as *adj.:* hair that has been chemically straightened and is worn smoothed down.

N double A C P: NAACP, or National Association for the Advancement of Colored People, an organization founded in 1909 to use legal means to end discrimination against African Americans.

Thirty pieces . . . less: allusion to the thirty pieces of silver that Judas Iscariot received for betraying Jesus Christ (Matthew 26:14–15).

***saucily** *adv.:* sassily; impertinently.

***taut** *adj.:* tense; strained.

Act Three

retrogression *n.:* backward movement; degeneration.

***flippancy** *n.:* playful impudence; mischievous impertinence.

***wrought** (alternative past form of *work*) *v.:* created; made.

Monsieur le petit bourgeois noir: French term referring to a black member of the *petite bourgeoisie,* a social class comprising the poorest business owners; the lower middle class.

Titan: In Greek mythology, the Titans are a race of giants. In modern usage, a titan is someone with a great deal of power.

ofay *adj.:* derogatory slang for a white person.

***gait** *n.:* manner of walking.

The Man: slang reference to a person or group of people in positions of authority used in the early 1950s to describe federal law-enforcement officers and quickly adopted by African Americans to refer to a white person or group of people in a position of authority.

***agitated** *adj.:* excited; frantic.

***epitaph** *n.:* short composition inscribed on a tombstone or otherwise used to remember the dead.

***negotiate** *v.:* bargain; arrange to conclude a business deal.

***groping** *v.* used as *adj.:* searching uncertainly; fumbling.

***reverie** *n.:* daydream; dreamlike inattention.

***bustling** *v.* used as *n.:* energetic activity; busyness.

Making Meanings: Act One

A Raisin in the Sun

First Thoughts

1. Think about the play's connection with Langston Hughes's poem "Harlem." Whose dreams are being deferred, and what do you predict will happen to them?

READING CHECK

Trace the significance of the insurance check in this act as it is transformed from an object of our curiosity to the central issue of the plot and a major source of **conflict.**

Shaping Interpretations

2. The audience's attention is held by people in conflict. Look at the opening scene up to Walter's exit. What subjects, large and small, do the characters argue or disagree about?
3. There has been a considerable build up to Mama's entrance, which is delayed until the middle of Scene 1. What do we learn about Mama before she appears? When she does make her entrance, Mama immediately shows us in small ways what kind of woman and mother she is. What does she do, and what do her actions reveal about her **character**?
4. It is important to understand and appreciate the strength of Mama's religious beliefs because they influence her decisions throughout the play. How does Hansberry show the strength of those beliefs?
5. Joseph Asagai allows the audience to view the Younger household from a different perspective. What does Asagai represent? How is he contrasted with what we know about George Murchison, Beneatha's other suitor?
6. What dramatic questions have been posed in the play so far? What are some possible answers to those questions?

Connecting with the Text

7. It has been said that in order to appreciate a play fully, the audience must believe in what is happening and care about the characters. Has the action in the play been believable so far? Which characters are you rooting for most, and why?

Extending the Text

8. Think about the way in which Mama speaks to Walter Lee toward the end of Act One. How do you think most adults would feel about being addressed in that fashion? Does your answer help you understand Walter better? Why?

Writing Opportunity

Expand your response into an essay that explores what other characters think of Walter Lee and how they make their thoughts known.

Name ______________________ Date ____________

Reading Strategies: Act One

A Raisin in the Sun

Organizing Information

Act One of *A Raisin in the Sun* introduces the Younger family, including the head of the household: Mama. **Information**—knowledge—about Mama's character helps to convey to the audience a sense of who she is and what she is like.

Use the following chart to organize information about Mama. Complete the chart with details from the play. Cite at least two details beneath each heading. Include quotations from the play. You might want to add to this chart as you continue to read the play. You also might adapt the chart so that you can organize information about other characters in the play.

Mama's Physical Appearance	Mama's Interests and Concerns
1. ______________________	1. ______________________
2. ______________________	2. ______________________
3. ______________________	3. ______________________
Mama's Background	**Mama's Actions**
1. ______________________	1. ______________________
2. ______________________	2. ______________________
3. ______________________	3. ______________________

FOLLOW-UP

- **What information on your chart do you think will give you an indication of how Mama makes her choices? Explain.**
- **Which of the actions that you listed do you think will become important in the play as it progresses? Why?**

Play Notes

Issue 1

Act One, *A Raisin in the Sun*

What Was Happening?

What was life like for African Americans in the 1950s? Consider these facts:

- The civil rights movement was in its infancy. Race-related lynchings, bombings, and arson still took place. Some local governments refused to obey antidiscrimination laws.
- Not until 1949 did any state ban all segregation of public accommodations. New Jersey and Connecticut passed laws to that effect year.
- Not until 1954 did the Supreme Court, in *Brown v. Board of Education of Topeka*, rule that segregation in public schools is unconstitutional.
- In 1957, New York State passed the first ordinance against discrimination in private as well as public housing.

INVESTIGATE • *What did the civil rights movement achieve in the 1950s?*

FOR YOUR READER'S LOG

What dreams or goals do you have? What can you do to make some of them come true?

Quotation Corner

Musing on Money

***Money speaks sense in a language all nations understand.* – Aphra Behn**

***Ready money is Aladdin's lamp.* – George Gordon, Lord Byron**

***The love of money is the root of all evil.* – The Bible: I Timothy 6:10**

Getting to Know the Yoruba

Nigeria, though far from Chicago, is still a presence in this play. The most populous country on the west coast of Africa, Nigeria was a British dependency when Hansberry's play opened, but it gained independence the next year.

The Yoruba live in the southwestern part of the country. They are well-known for their crafts, including terra-cotta and brass sculpture, ivory and brass jewelry, and wooden masks. Most Yoruba traders are women, and many Yoruba women hold important titles as chieftains.

When a Yoruba child is just a few days old, the parents hold a naming ceremony, known as *lkose w'aye*, "stepping into the world." A Yoruba healer chooses a name (Honor Comes Home, for example) that describes the child's soul, and then offers the parents advice on rearing the child.

INVESTIGATE • *What does your name mean?*

The Word PLACE

Ghetto

Does the word *ghetto* bring a distinctly American picture to your mind? Actually, the word ghetto was first used in Venice in 1516. It comes from the Italian word for *foundry*. In 1516, an area that had once been the site of an iron foundry was set aside as a Jewish settlement. It was shut off from the rest of the city and was guarded by Christian watchmen. Jewish ghettos—walled-off neighborhoods whose gates were locked at night—were the law in many European cities from the mid-1400s until the late 1800s. The ghetto in this play has no literal walls or locked gates, but its residents feel a strong sense of confinement.

Name ______________________ Date ______________

Choices: Act One

A Raisin in the Sun

Building Your Portfolio

ART

All Set

Sketch a possible set for the first act of *A Raisin in the Sun*. Remember: The play opens in the living room, the focus of the set, but a kitchen, bedrooms, and a hallway are also visible. How much of those parts of the apartment need to be seen? If you wish, exchange sketches with a partner, and evaluate each other's set design.

READING STRATEGIES

Raisin Questions

Have your teacher organize the class into several small groups. With the other members of your group, write five questions about Act One of *A Raisin in the Sun*. Some questions can be about details of the plot. Others can be about conflicts or problems in this part of the play. Write each question on an index card and its answer on the back—five cards in all. With your teacher's help, gather the cards and organize the class into two teams. After the teacher or a student reads each question aloud, have a scorekeeper award one point to the team that answers it correctly. If you wish, expand this activity to cover the entire play.

VOCABULARY DEVELOPMENT

Character Words

Now that you have met Hansberry's characters, how would you describe them? Choose three characters, and list three words that you think describe each one. If English is your second language, write words from your first language. Share your lists, and explain why you think your choices are appropriate.

Consider This . . .

No—there's something come down between me and them that don't let us understand each other and I don't know what it is.

What do you think has "come down" between Mama and her children? Explain your answer.

Writing Follow-up: Problem-Solution

Write a brief letter to Mama. Show that you understand her problem and her feelings about it. As a friend, suggest at least one change that you think might improve matters in the Younger home.

Play Notes

Create an activity based on **Play Notes, Issue 1.** Here is a suggestion.

- Read and summarize the text of the Supreme Court's decision in *Brown v. Board of Education of Topeka*, written by Chief Justice Earl Warren.

Making Meanings: Act Two

A Raisin in the Sun

First Thoughts

1. Do you think Mama did the right thing with her money? Explain.

READING CHECK

Summarize the main events in Scenes 1, 2, and 3.

Shaping Interpretations

2. In Scene 1, why does George address Walter as "Prometheus"? Explain the **allusion.** (You might check Play Notes, Issue 2, or do some original research.)
3. Walter asks Ruth, "What is it gets into people ought to be close?" When they try to talk about why they are having problems, Walter and Ruth reach no conclusion. What do you think the playwright wants us to understand about the cause of their problems?
4. Beneatha is a serious character, but she becomes comic through her excesses. Discuss how she can be seen as a comic **character.** Is Beneatha a believable character, or is she a stereotype? Explain your answer.
5. To whom does Mama first tell her news in Scene 1? What is her **motivation** for doing that?
6. How would you describe Lindner's **tone** as he talks with the Youngers? How does that tone contrast with his message?
7. Scene 3 is full of reversals, in which sudden shifts take place in the fortunes of the main characters. Discuss the reversals in this scene. How does the mood of this scene change from its beginning to its end?

Writing Opportunity

Write at least one paragraph discussing Lindner's words in more detail. Does Lindner understand the mixed message in his presentation? How do you think Hansberry wants us to feel about him?

Connecting with the Text

8. How do you feel about the various characters at this point in the play? Are you rooting for any particular character? Have your sympathies switched from one character to another? Explain.

Challenging the Text

9. In the original production and some early editions of *A Raisin in the Sun,* the encounter with Mrs. Johnson is left out. What is her purpose in Act Two? Do you think the play is hurt by the omission? Why or why not?

Name ______________________________ Date ______________

Reading Strategies: Act Two

A Raisin in the Sun

Drawing Conclusions

Think about the ways in which Mama, Walter, and Beneatha interact during Act Two. Draw some conclusions about their feelings toward each other. (Consider the entire act, not just its beginning or end.)

For the arrows outside this triangle, describe the feelings that the character named at the beginning of each arrow has for the character at the end of the arrow. Do the same for the arrows inside the triangle.

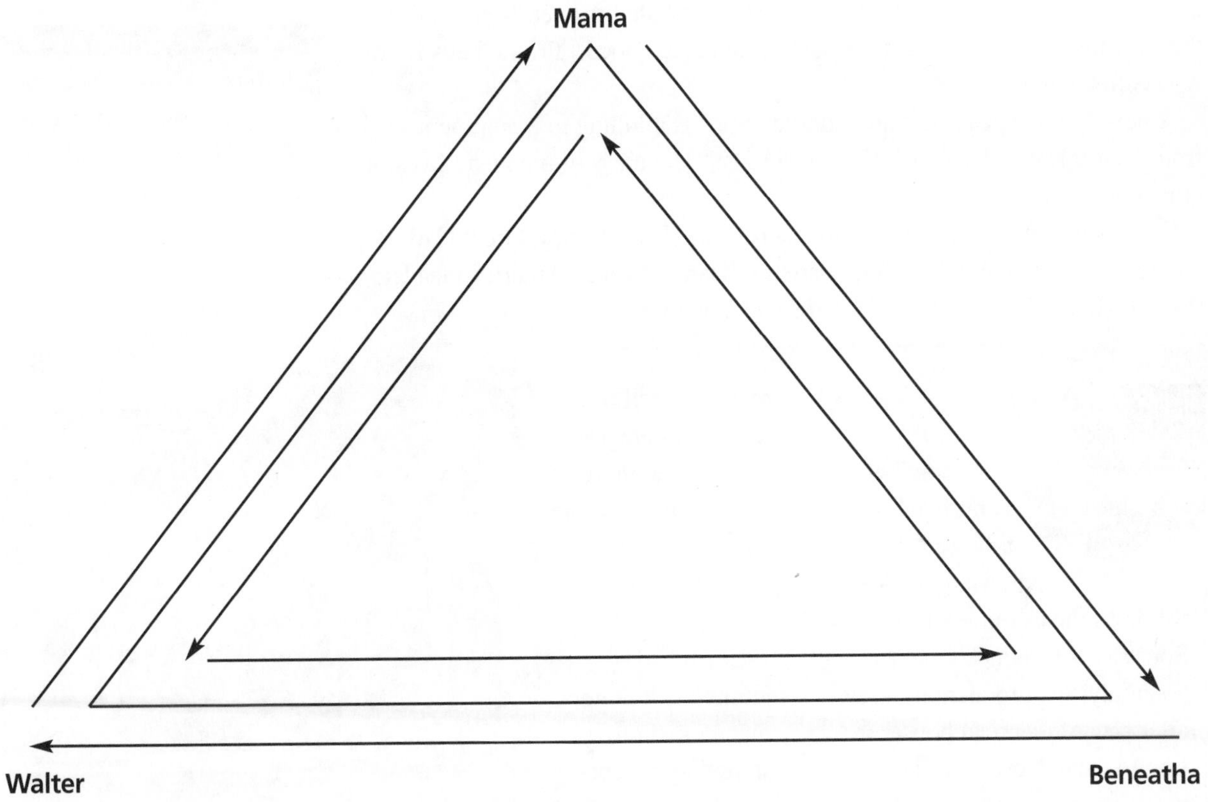

FOLLOW-UP

- **How has the relationship between Mama and Walter changed from their relationship in Act One? What further change is implied at the end of Act Two?**

  ____

  ____

- **In your opinion, how are Ruth and Travis, the other two family members, affected by these characters' feelings toward each other?**

  ____

  ____

Play Notes

Issue 2

Act Two, *A Raisin in the Sun*

Master of Allusion

Who is Prometheus? What is "quiet desperation"? These are just a few of the **allusions** (references to details from history, literature, religion, and other branches of culture) that pepper Act Two.

According to Greek mythology, Prometheus was a Titan (giant) who stole fire from the gods and gave it to humans. His punishment? Zeus chained him to a rock, where each day an eagle came and ate his liver. (Zeus caused the liver to regrow each night, so the torture never ended.) Prometheus finally was freed by Hercules.

A person who speaks of "quiet desperation" is alluding to a comment from Henry David Thoreau's *Walden* (1854): "The mass of men lead lives of quiet desperation."

Other allusions in Act Two are to entertainers (Pearl Bailey, Greta Garbo), movie characters (Mrs. Miniver, Scarlett O'Hara), African American leaders (Booker T. Washington, W. E. B. Du Bois), and more.

For Your Reader's Log

If you could have a heart-to-heart talk with a character in this play, whom would you choose? What would you say?

History in a Nutshell:

House Sense

A "boom" in suburban housing followed World War II. Many builders followed the example of Levitt & Sons, who introduced the near assembly-line production of row after row of identical houses in Long Island, New York. These houses were priced at $7,000 to $8,000. Levitt refused to sell to African Americans for many years. His reason, he maintained, was economic: "I have come to know that if we sell one house to a Negro family, then 90 to 95 percent of our white customers will not buy into the community."

Levitt had numerous imitators, many of whom started to cut corners for greater profit. A person shopping for a house in the suburbs would have to look carefully to find a house with proper basic construction.

INVESTIGATE • *What are the pros and cons of living in the suburbs today?*

NAACP

The National Association for the Advancement of Colored People (NAACP), established in 1910 to work for the end of racial discrimination and segregation, was formed as the direct result of the 1908 lynching of two blacks in Springfield, Illinois. As early as 1915, the NAACP was able to organize a partially successful boycott of an offensive movie, but early efforts were directed, successfully, against lynchings. By the 1950s, with this worst example of racism largely eliminated, the NAACP could turn to other civil rights issues.

Name ______________________ Date ______________

Choices: Act Two

A Raisin in the Sun

Building Your Portfolio

MUSIC

Folk Focus

Nigerian folk music opens Act Two in a powerful way. Find a recording of Nigerian or other African folk songs. Choose a song that reminds you of this play in some way. Then play or perform the song for the class and explain your choice.

CREATIVE WRITING/PERFORMANCE

History Speaks!

In Act Two, Scene 2, Mama and Mrs. Johnson have a heated exchange about "old Booker T." Booker T. Washington (1856–1915) felt that the best way for African Americans to advance was through vocational education. He implied that African Americans should earn their rights as citizens by proving, over time, that they could be successful financially. A different view came from W. E. B. Du Bois (1868–1963), one of the founders of the NAACP (and one of Hansberry's mentors). Du Bois urged African Americans to be politically active, without delay. He also supported broad education that went beyond vocational training. What might Washington and Du Bois say about the events that are unfolding in *A Raisin in the Sun?* With a partner, write and present a pair of dramatic monologues—one from Washington, one from Du Bois. Have these two leaders approve or disapprove of characters or actions. Also have them offer advice that they think will improve the lives of the Youngers (or the lives of the people that the Youngers represent).

CRITICAL WRITING

Funny and Sad

In his review of *A Raisin in the Sun* on its opening at the Ethel Barrymore Theater in 1959, critic Brooks Atkinson wrote that the situations in the play range from "hilarious" to "painful." In a paragraph explain why you agree or disagree with Atkinson's remarks. Think about the scenes that have made you laugh and the scenes or situations that were painful.

Consider This . . .

What do you think you are going to gain by moving into a neighborhood where you just aren't wanted. . . . You just can't force people to change their hearts, son.

What do the Youngers hope to gain by making the move? Do you think their hope is strong enough to overcome people's unwillingness to change their hearts?

Writing Follow-up: Persuasion

Write an editorial that urges people at Clybourne Park to "change their hearts." Explain what their community would gain by welcoming neighbors like the Youngers.

Play Notes

Create an activity based on **Play Notes, Issue 2.** Here are two suggestions.

- Make a sketch of your dreamhouse, then find one like it in a real-estate listing to see how much it might cost.
- Research these allusions to the Bible: *forbidden fruit, a lamb to the slaughter, turn the other cheek.*

Making Meanings: Act Three

A Raisin in the Sun

First Thoughts

1. How did you feel about the family's decision to move to the new neighborhood?

READING CHECK

The scene with Mr. Lindner is the climax of the play. What happens during this scene to end our doubts about the Younger family's decision?

Shaping Interpretations

2. Think about Asagai's "I live the answer" speech. How does it address Beneatha's immediate concerns? How does it underscore one **theme** of this play?
3. When Mama starts talking about canceling the move, Ruth's **tone** becomes frantic. Why is she so upset?
4. Walter claims that he will feel like a man when he can buy the things that Lindner's money would make possible. What **irony** lies in his claim?
5. How does Mama stand up for Walter when Beneatha condemns him? How does she try to make him stand up for himself?

Writing Opportunity

Compose an essay response to the first part of this question. Explain how Mama's speech affects the reader's view of her character and helps express a key idea of the play.

6. Discuss the use of **suspense** in Act Three. What do we fear will happen? How does Hansberry draw out the action so that our suspense is heightened?
7. In literature, a **dynamic character** changes and grows as a result of his or her experiences. A **static character** remains essentially the same from beginning to end. Which characters in this play are dynamic? Which are static? Briefly explain your choices.
8. Both Mama and Walter seem defeated for a while in Act Three. However, we know from the play's general tone that it cannot end in defeat for these good people. In spite of their apparent defeat and despair, we sense that the playwright is preparing us for another reversal. What is it that rouses each character from defeat to the joyful, triumphant note on which the play ends?

Extending the Text

9. Movie director Spike Lee writes, "We all have to ask ourselves, have things gotten any better than when the play was written? I have to say I think they've gotten worse." Tell why you agree or disagree with this statement. Are the issues that Hansberry raises still pertinent in the United States, or is the play outdated?

Name ____________________ Date ____________

Reading Strategies: Act Three

A Raisin in the Sun

Evaluating Cause and Effect

A **cause** is what makes something happen. An **effect** is what happens. Causes and effects may be external or internal events. Some effects have more than one cause; some causes have more than one effect; and, of course, some effects become causes of later effects.

Complete the following cause-and-effect chart about the events in Act Three of *A Raisin in the Sun*.

CAUSE	EFFECT
1. As a child, Beneatha saw how a friend was helped by medical care.	**1.** ____________________
2. ____________________	**2.** When Asagai leaves, Beneatha is confused.
3. ____________________	**3.** Ruth promises to work twenty hours a day to make extra money.
4. Beneatha announces that Walter is "no brother of mine."	**4.** ____________________
5. Mama tells Travis to stay in the apartment.	**5.** ____________________
6. ____________________	**6.** Walter refuses Lindner's offer.
7. ____________________	**7.** Mama decides that Walter has "finally come into his manhood."

FOLLOW-UP: This play begins with a poem that asks, "What happens to a dream deferred?" Think about the cause-and-effect statements on your completed chart. Briefly identify and explain which statements you think deal most directly with that question.

____

____

Play Notes

Issue 3

Act Three, *A Raisin in the Sun*

It's a Fact

What would you do if you found out that you couldn't move into your new house because your new neighbors had agreed that "people like you" weren't going to live among them?

That's what happened to Carl Hansberry, Lorraine Hansberry's father, in 1938: Residents of an all-white neighborhood in which he had bought a house sued to keep him out. He fought back in court, and he refused to give up. Finally, in 1940, the case of *Hansberry v. Lee* went before the Supreme Court. Civil-rights advocates wanted the Court to declare private agreements, known as restrictive covenants, unconstitutional. The Court decided in Hansberry's favor, but on a technicality; restrictive covenants would not be ruled unconstitutional until 1948. Still, the experience gave Lorraine Hansberry the idea for *A Raisin in the Sun,* and many readers consider the play a tribute to her father.

For Your Reader's Log

What do you consider to be the hardest change of mind that you have ever made?

On the Money

What plans the Youngers had for their $10,000, and how the loss of much of that amount hurt them! It's no wonder: At that time, $10,000 was double the yearly salary of the average American and about $7,000 above the poverty line for a family of four. In an era when many new cars cost less than $2,500, a lump sum of $10,000 could go far.

The Word Place

Epithets

"Sticks and stones may break my bones but . . . words will never hurt me!" Beneatha says in Act Two. Some words, though, are meant to hurt. **Epithets**—derogatory names—are among them. In Act Two, the epithets *crackers* and *peckerwoods* are used to disparage white people. Act Three adds to the list with *ofay, The Man, Captain Boss,* and a few others. These words are hard to hear, of course, even though they're not said directly to the people to whom they refer. They capture, however, the anger at the discrimination that Hansberry's characters face every day.

INVESTIGATE

- *How must society change before people stop feeling the need to vent their anger by using epithets?*

Name ______________________________ Date ______________

Choices: Act Three

A Raisin in the Sun

Building Your Portfolio

CRITICAL WRITING

Universal Significance

Hansberry has said about playwriting: "I believe that one of the most sound ideas in dramatic writing is that in order to create the universal, you must pay very great attention to the specific."

Do you think that *A Raisin in the Sun* says something universal about human beings? Or do you think that the play focuses in such realistic detail—on a specific family living at a particular time on the South Side of Chicago—that it fails in its attempt to say something universal about human beings? Discuss these questions in a brief essay.

CRITICAL WRITING

Do Yourself Proud

In the characters of Beneatha and Asagai, Hansberry deals with the relationship of African Americans to their African heritage. How important do you think it is for a person to know about his or her cultural, ethnic, racial, or religious background? Is pride in one's heritage necessary for a person to have a positive sense of identity and self-esteem? Or should assimilation be the goal of Americans? In a brief essay, explore what you think about these questions, and give reasons to support your answers.

PERFORMANCE

Bring It to Life

With a group, prepare a scene of the play for performance. You can act out the scene, or you can do a group reading. In a reading, the performers do not have to memorize the lines; they read from the script. Lighting and costumes might be used in a reading to help create atmosphere. Whichever kind of presentation you decide on, you will have to appoint a director and prepare scripts for your actors.

Consider This . . .

When you starts measuring somebody, measure him right, child, measure him right. Make sure you done taken into account what hills and valleys he come through before he got to wherever he is.

Why does Mama stand up for Walter Lee at this bleak moment? How is her devotion justified at the end of the play?

Writing Follow-up: Cause and Effect

How do "hills and valleys" make people what they are? Write either a character sketch or a reflective essay in which you show how "hills and valleys" have affected a person you know—or you yourself.

Play Notes

Create an activity based on **Play Notes, Issue 3.** Here are two suggestions.

- Write an editorial that explains why, in your opinion, restrictive policies harm rather than help a community.
- Compare and contrast the value of $10,000 in the early 1950s with its value today.

Name ______________________ Date ____________

Play Review

A Raisin in the Sun

MAJOR CHARACTERS

Use the chart below to keep track of the characters in this play. Each time you come across a new character, write the character's name and the number of the page on which the character first appears. Then, jot down a brief description. Add information about the characters as you read. Put a star next to the name of each main character.

NAME OF CHARACTER	DESCRIPTION

FOLLOW-UP: Construct a paragraph that discusses the sequence or significance of information recorded in this Play Organizer.

Name ______________________ Date ______________

Play Review *(cont.)*

A Raisin in the Sun

SETTING

Time ______________________

Most important place(s) ______________________

One effect of setting on plot, theme, or character ______________________

PLOT

List key events from the play.

- ______________________
- ______________________
- ______________________
- ______________________
- ______________________
- ______________________

Use your list to identify the plot elements below. Add other events as necessary.

Major conflict / problem ______________________

Turning point / climax ______________________

Resolution / denouement ______________________

MAJOR THEMES

- ______________________
- ______________________
- ______________________

Name ________________________________ Date ____________

Literary Elements Worksheet 1

A Raisin in the Sun

Character and Characterization

A **static character** is one who does not change much during the course of a play. A **dynamic character,** on the other hand, does change in some important ways. Walter Lee Younger is a dynamic character, and he is characterized in several ways.

Complete this diagram with details, quotations, or other notes to show how Walter Lee changes over the course of the play.

WALTER LEE—AT THE BEGINNING	WALTER LEE—AT THE END
What he says:	What he says:
What other characters say about him:	What other characters say about him:
What the stage directions say about him:	What the stage directions say about him:
What he does:	What he does:

FOLLOW-UP: Choose a static character from the play. Briefly describe how Hansberry lets us know what the character is like.

____

____

____

Name ______________________ Date ______________

Literary Elements Worksheet 2

A Raisin in the Sun

External and Internal Conflict

The chance to fulfill their dreams for a better life creates several conflicts, or clashes, for members of the Younger family.

Within each box, summarize an external conflict between the characters named next to the arrows. If the same name appears by both arrows, summarize an internal conflict that that character faces.

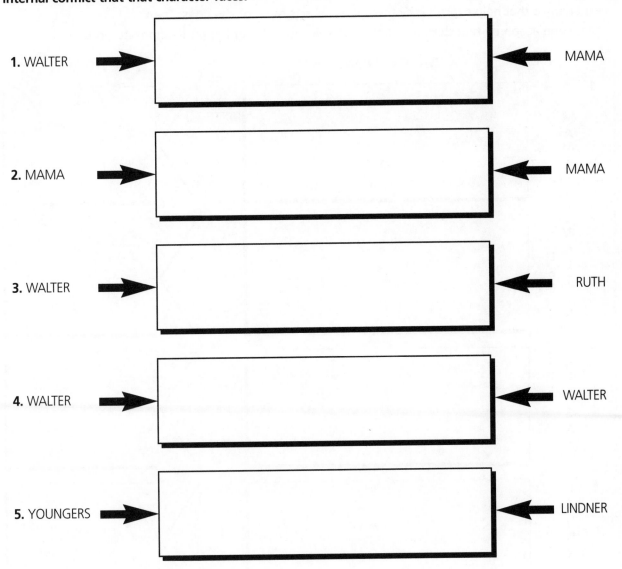

1. WALTER → [ ] ← MAMA

2. MAMA → [ ] ← MAMA

3. WALTER → [ ] ← RUTH

4. WALTER → [ ] ← WALTER

5. YOUNGERS → [ ] ← LINDNER

FOLLOW-UP

- **Describe another internal or external conflict that you see in the play (for example, Walter/Beneatha or Ruth/Ruth).**

____

____

Name ______________________________ Date ______________

Literary Elements Worksheet 3

A Raisin in the Sun

Motivation

Motivations are personal qualities, feelings, and experiences that push a character toward certain habits and decisions. For example, Beneatha's desire to express herself leads her to try one hobby after another. It also sparks her interest in her African heritage (and in Joseph Asagai).

For each character listed, jot down two of the personal qualities, feelings, and/or experiences that help explain why this character acts as he or she does. Then name one action by that character that you think shows his or her motivations at work.

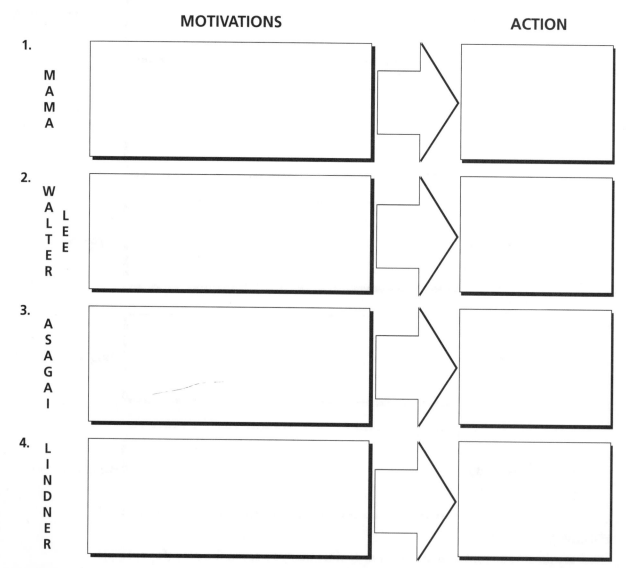

	MOTIVATIONS		ACTION
1. MAMA		→	
2. WALTER LEE		→	
3. ASAGAI		→	
4. LINDNER		→	

FOLLOW-UP

- **Look back at your responses. Explain how one character's motivations bring him or her into conflict with another character. (Give one specific example.)**
- **Whose motivation do you sympathize with the most? Explain.**

Name ______________________________ Date ______________

Vocabulary Worksheet

A Raisin in the Sun

A. In the space provided, write the letter of the word that most nearly defines each word in bold type. (All items are from *A Raisin in the Sun*.)

_____ 1. And his woman say—*(in utter anguish as he brings his fists down on his thighs)*—Your eggs is getting cold! *Here the word* **anguish** *means*

a. amazement
b. rage
c. heartache
d. merriment

_____ 2. How often I have looked at you and said, "Ah—so this is what the New World hath finally wrought . . ." *Here the word* **wrought** *means*

a. created
b. judged
c. chosen
d. worshipped

_____ 3. *He leaps up and clasps his father around the middle with his legs, and they face each other in mutual appreciation. . . . Here the word* **mutual** *means*

a. shared
b. unrestrained
c. deep
d. sincere

_____ 4. *She is one of those women of a certain grace and beauty who wear it so unobtrusively that it takes a while to notice. Here the word* **unobtrusively** *means*

a. naturally
b. inconspicuously
c. gladly
d. easily

_____ 5. MAMA *and* RUTH *look at each other and burst into raucous laughter. Here the word* **raucous** *means*

a. shared
b. sudden
c. relieved
d. loud

_____ 6. *He is a lean, intense young man . . . and always in his voice there is a quality of indictment.* Here the *word* **indictment** *means*

a. curiosity
b. complaint
c. helplessness
d. guiltiness

_____ 7. In my time we was worried about not being lynched and getting to the North if we could . . . *Here the word* **lynched** *means*

a. separated
b. sold
c. murdered
d. abused

_____ 8. Well—with whom do I negotiate? You, Mrs. Younger, or your son here? *Here the word* **negotiate** *means*

a. speak
b. collaborate
c. argue
d. bargain

_____ 9. *An imploring quality in her voice, her manner, makes her almost like a girl now. Here the word* **imploring** *means*

a. pleading
b. innocent
c. desperate
d. playful

Vocabulary Worksheet *(cont.)*

A Raisin in the Sun

_____ **10.** *She waits a long time, and then with resignation starts to put away her things. Here the word* **resignation** *means*

a. resentment
b. hesitation
c. determination
d. acceptance

_____ **11.** *Then she starts to rise, bringing her fists down with vigor, the radiance spreading from cheek to cheek again. Here the word* **vigor** *means*

a. emotion
b. rejoicing
c. vitality
d. finality

_____ **12.** *There is a profound, simple groping quality in his speech. Here the word* **groping** *means*

a. angry
b. fumbling
c. persuasive
d. demanding

B. Write the word from the box that best completes each sentence.

oppression	furtively	exasperated
sobriety	permeated	revelation
flippancy	gait	agitated

_____ **13.** The sound of running water from the hallway bathroom ____________ the Youngers' small apartment.

_____ **14.** With a frown and a(n) ____________ sigh, Ruth listened once again to Walter's complaints about life.

_____ **15.** Walter then slipped out ____________ to meet with Bobo and Willy.

_____ **16.** What a(n) ____________ it has been for him to learn what Willy did with their money!

_____ **17.** Now Walter seems so ____________ that he may try anything to get more money.

C. Match each word in the left-hand column with its meaning in the right-hand column.

_____ **18.** taut
_____ **19.** drily
_____ **20.** bustling
_____ **21.** saucily
_____ **22.** reverie
_____ **23.** exuberant
_____ **24.** reflective
_____ **25.** epitaph

a. meditative
b. daydream
c. uninhibited
d. sassily
e. matter-of-factly
f. energetic activity
g. memorial phrase
h. tense

Name ______________________ Date ______________

Play Projects

A Raisin in the Sun

Writing About the Play

STUDY GUIDE

Top Ten List

Make a list titled "The Top Ten Things to Remember About *A Raisin in the Sun*." You can describe characters, quote their words, name key dramatic moments, or note themes or other important ideas from the play. Compare your list with lists from a few classmates. Which items appear on several lists?
(Critical Writing)

POEM

An Apt Epigraph

Write an original poem that could be used as a new epigraph—an opening quotation—for *A Raisin in the Sun*, as Lorraine Hansberry used Langston Hughes's "Harlem." Your poem might address one of the age-old themes dealt with in the play: for example, human beings' inhumanity to one another; the frustrations of being unable to achieve a dream; or people's ability to summon the courage to overcome adversity.
(Creative Writing)

ONE-ACT PLAY

406 Clybourne Street

When one critic spoke of this play's "happy ending," Lorraine Hansberry responded, "If he thinks that's a happy ending, I invite him to come live in one of the communities where the Youngers are going!" What will happen to the Youngers in their new home? On your own or with a partner, write a sequel to *A Raisin in the Sun*—a one-act play that shows how the move turns out. Try to capture the characters as you understand them. Show what has become of their dreams. If possible, stage a production of your play.
(Creative Writing)

INTERVIEW

In the Spotlight

Get together with two classmates and make a list of questions that you wish you could ask Lorraine Hansberry about *A Raisin in the Sun*. Then, hold a discussion. One person should ask a question; the second, as Hansberry, should answer it; the third should agree or disagree with that answer and explain why. Switch roles until you have answered all the questions on your list. Afterward, discuss how this activity gives you a better understanding of *A Raisin in the Sun*. *(Creative/Critical Writing)*

Name ______________________ Date ____________

Cross-Curricular Connections

SOCIAL STUDIES

Back to the Past

The Youngers are challenged to think about their African heritage and about current events in Africa. Are such thoughts important to the play? Gather some information about one of the following topics from the play:

- ancient African technology
- the Ashanti or Songhay (Songhai) empire
- African folk arts
- the modern independence movement in African countries
- the importance of Chaka or of Jomo Kenyatta

Prepare a short (3–5 minute) oral report. In it, offer some factual information about your topic; then share and defend your opinion about the topic's importance to the characters, themes, or events in the play.

FINE ARTS

Raisin, the Musical

In 1973, *Raisin*—a musical based on *A Raisin in the Sun*, with music by Judd Woldin and lyrics by Robert Brittain—opened on Broadway. It won the Tony Award for Best Musical. Listen to the original cast recording of *Raisin*. (You can probably find it at a library.) Then play some excerpts for the class and share your thoughts about them. You might focus on three types of songs:

- Songs that capture key passages of dialogue (such as "You Done Right," Walter's angry response to Mama's purchase of the house; and "Measure the Valleys," Mama's "measure him right" speech)
- Songs that expand on other elements (such as "Whose Angry Little Man," Ruth's song to Travis)
- Songs that add new elements (such as "He Come Down This Morning," a gospel song sung at Mama's church)

MATHEMATICS

Money Matters

Use microfilm holdings or other library resources to study some advertisements in newspapers from the early 1950s. Jot down prices of some common items (such as a dozen eggs, a pair of shoes, train fares for vacations, or the average cost of college tuition) and determine what an average paycheck might have been able to buy. Show how much $10,000 meant to the Youngers. Then create a budget proposal to show how they might get the most for this money. How might such a plan have affected the dreams and conflicts in the play?

Name ______________________________ Date ______________

Multimedia and Internet Connections

NOTE: Check with your teacher about school policies on accessing Internet sites. If a Web site named here is not available, use key words to locate a similar site.

FILM: REVIEW

Viewing and Verdicts

Both the 1961 film adaptation of *A Raisin in the Sun* and its 1989 made-for-television version (recommended by Robert Nemiroff, Hansberry's husband and literary executor) are available on videocassette. Watch one presentation of the entire play, or watch the same scenes as presented in both versions. What differences do you see between the film version(s) and the play that you have read? What are the strengths and/or weaknesses of the performance(s) that you have viewed?

TELEVISION: NEWS MAGAZINE

Tonight's Feature

Television news magazines feature a mix of news stories and human-interest features. With several classmates, plan a segment about the Youngers' move to Clybourne Park for such a news magazine. For example, reenact the Youngers' arrival, and have someone interview both them and their new white neighbors. You also might seek comments from a representative of the NAACP, get background information from a civil-rights lawyer, or ask a local politician for his or her analysis of the situation. Perform the segment live, or videotape it and watch it with your class.

INTERNET: RESEARCH

Housing Discrimination Today

Is discrimination in housing still a problem? Use the Internet to find out. Try a key word search, or visit sites such as the following:

- The NAACP Home Page (http://www.naacp.org)
- The National Fair Housing Alliance (http://www.incacorp.com/nfha)
- National Fair Housing Advocate Online (http://www.fairhousing.com)

As you share your findings in a class discussion, talk about the options that the Youngers might have if their story were set in today's world.

VIDEO: TELEPLAY

Bringing It to Life

With a group of classmates, prepare two passages from *A Raisin in the Sun* as if your presentation were to be televised. Discuss the reasons for choosing the passages you want to present. (You may want to include a video "host" to explain the connection on film.) Next, choose a director, cast the parts, and block out the presentation with one or two videographers. Rehearse and then enact the material, with cameras rolling. How does your understanding of Hansberry's play change when you are presenting it instead of reading it?

INTERNET: RESEARCH

Hansberry Online

See what information you discover by using *Lorraine Hansberry* in a key word search on the Internet. For example, you might locate biographies, information about the Lorraine Hansberry Theater in San Francisco, ads for local productions of *A Raisin in the Sun*, or databases devoted to study of her works. Be sure to share what you find—and what you learned about Internet research as you looked.

Introducing the Connections

The **Connections** at the end of the HRW LIBRARY edition of *A Raisin in the Sun* create the opportunity for students to relate it's themes to other genres, times, and places and to their own lives. The following chart will facilitate your use of these additional works. Succeeding pages offer **Making Meanings** questions to stimulate student response.

Selection	Summary, Connection to Play
A Letter from the Playwright Lorraine Hansberry *personal letter*	Writing to her mother as *A Raisin in the Sun* prepares for its opening in New Haven, Lorraine Hansberry expresses her worries and hopes and characterizes her drama as "a play that tells the truth about people, Negroes, and life."
Chicago: Southside Summers *from* To Be Young, Gifted and Black Lorraine Hansberry *documentary drama*	The portion of the semi-autobiographical work included here briefly describes Hansberry's childhood and the neighborhood in which *A Raisin in the Sun* is set—the neighborhood in which Hansberry was born. The playwright remembers her siblings and parents, with special attention to her father. The excerpt concludes with a letter that Hansberry wrote to *The New York Times,* a letter that bitterly recalls a real-life inspiration for *A Raisin in the Sun* and offers a warning about the state of race relations in 1964.
My Dungeon Shook: Letter to My Nephew on the One Hundredth Anniversary of Emancipation letter written by James Baldwin *historical document*	On the centennial of the Emancipation Proclamation, James Baldwin writes to his teenage nephew. His letter charges the United States and its people with the blind destruction of hundreds of thousands of lives because of racial prejudice. Baldwin urges his nephew to survive, to understand what white people mean when they use words such as *acceptance* and *integration,* and to "force our [white] brothers to see themselves as they are."
Home *from* Maud Martha Gwendolyn Brooks *novel*	This story presents an African American family who are having trouble meeting their mortgage payments and fear that they are about to lose their home. Though they try to put the best face they can upon that possibility, they are jubilant when they learn that they have been granted an extension and will not have to leave the home that means more to them than perhaps they realized.

Introducing the Connections *(cont.)*

Selection	Summary, Connection to Play
2239 North 16th Street *from* Sweet Summer: Growing Up with and Without My Dad Bebe Moore Campbell *memoir*	Campbell recalls her childhood home and school with vivid detail and often with humor. At the heart of this excerpt from her memoir, however, is a classroom incident in which Campbell, resentful of the lives of her more privileged white classmates, lashes out with a threatening bluff that causes the principal to brand her with a racial stereotype.
Everything That Rises Must Converge Flannery O'Connor *short story*	Julian, a college graduate with no apparent ambition, lives with his mother who decries the "mess" that the world is in because of the "rise" of African Americans and the desegregation around her. He detests her prejudice and takes every opportunity to tell her so. In fact, both of them have built quite different fantasy worlds for themselves. Julian's fantasies are shattered, however, when his mother clashes with an African American with whom they have shared a bus ride. As a result, she retreats into her fantasy world—perhaps permanently—leaving Julian to reflect upon his past attitudes.
The March to Montgomery *from* From Camelot to Kent State John Lewis *memoir*	In this excerpt from his memoir about his experiences in the 1960s civil-rights movement, John Lewis describes the march from Selma to Montgomery, Alabama, led by Martin Luther King, Jr. The march had a slow start; many people, including Lewis, were injured. By the end, however, this powerful event changed history, inspiring President Johnson to speak out on civil rights as he had never done before and compelling the entire nation to listen and to think about Dr. King's message.

Exploring the Connections

Making Meanings

A Letter from the Playwright

Connecting with the Play

Which **characters** in *A Raisin in the Sun* display "the very essence of human dignity"? How?

1. What does Hansberry imply about her hopes for the people who have worked hard to bring her play to the stage?
2. In what way does Hansberry hope that her play will change stereotypical thinking about African Americans?
3. Describe a story that you have read or seen on film that you think "tells the truth about people." What "truth" does it tell?

Reading Check

a. Under what circumstances is Hansberry writing this letter, and to whom?

b. According to Hansberry, what is *A Raisin in the Sun* "supposed to say"?

Chicago: Southside Summers

Connecting with the Play

The conclusion of this selection draws special attention to the last line of the play's **epigraph.** What "explosions" occur in *A Raisin in the Sun?*

1. How does Hansberry characterize her parents? Her brothers and sisters?
2. Think about the **images** in Hansberry's letter to the editor. What makes them so effective?
3. If you were to "put down the stuff" of your life, what image of yourself do you think would shine through?
4. *To Be Young, Gifted and Black* is a collection of various kinds of documents. In your opinion, is this an effective way to capture someone's life and personality? Why, or why not?

Reading Check

a. In Hansberry's family, what two things "were never to be betrayed"?

b. As Hansberry remembers her father, what realization surprises her?

c. Why does Hansberry write a letter to the editor of *The New York Times?*

My Dungeon Shook: Letter to My Nephew on the One Hundredth Anniversary of Emancipation

Connecting with the Play

How do Baldwin's words reflect Big Walter's belief that God gave children to African Americans to make the parents' dreams seem worthwhile?

1. If you could ask James Baldwin some questions about this letter, what would you want to know?
2. Why does Baldwin think of the United States and of Americans as criminals?
3. Baldwin states that this is the sixth time he has tried to write this letter. Why do you suppose he had such a hard time writing to his nephew?

Reading Check

a. What occasion has prompted this letter from Baldwin to his nephew?

b. How would Baldwin define *integration?*

Making Meanings

Home

Connecting with the Play

Would *Home* be a good title for Hansberry's play? Defend your answer.

1. Did the **resolution** of this story surprise you? Why or why not?
2. How would you describe the **mood** or **atmosphere** of this story?
3. At the end of the story, how has Helen's opinion of the house changed? What do her thoughts suggest about the **theme** of Brooks's story?

READING CHECK

a. What problem is Papa trying to solve?

b. What do the other members of the household do while they wait for his return?

2239 North 16th Street

Connecting with the Play

How does the attitude that Jennie G. shows express itself in *A Raisin in the Sun?* Does any character in the play resemble her? Explain.

1. How does the last sentence affect your interpretation of the story?
2. In general, what do the women in young Bebe's home want from her? At school, how does Miss Bradley reinforce this idea?
3. What **motivation** for Bebe's emotional outburst is implied in the story?

READING CHECK

a. What makes Bebe's house different from the neighboring houses?

b. Why does Bebe's mother enroll her at Logan Elementary School?

c. Why does Bebe get into trouble at the school?

Everything That Rises Must Converge

Making Meanings

Connecting with the Play

Like Mama and Ruth Younger, Julian wants to move. What motivation do they all share?

1. Do you think that Julian's mother deserved her fate? Why or why not?
2. Why do you suppose Julian treats his mother so cruelly? Why do you suppose she continues to make excuses for him?
3. Julian complains that his mother lives in a world of **fantasy.** In what fantasies does he indulge, even if he does not realize it?
4. What do you think will happen to Julian and his mother after the final scene in this story?

Reading Check

a. Why is Julian traveling with his mother?
b. What is his mother's attitude to African Americans and to desegregation?
c. What happens when Julian's mother tries to give Carver a penny?

The March to Montgomery

Connecting with the Play

The march from Selma to Montgomery took place in 1965, eight years after Hansberry wrote *A Raisin in the Sun.* What would the Youngers have thought of the march? Do you think an event of that magnitude would have been possible in 1957? Why or why not?

1. What details does the author use to make his eyewitness account so powerful?
2. What is the turning point in the march? What made it such a success?
3. What are the lasting effects of the march to Montgomery? How did it change history?

Reading Check

a. Why were voting rights an important issue for the civil-rights movement?
b. How did the author sustain a concussion?
c. Why was the "second phase" of the march so "meaningful"?
d. What did the military make possible during the second phase of the march?

Name ______________________________ Date ______________

TEST PART I: OBJECTIVE QUESTIONS

In the space provided, mark each true statement *T* and each false statement *F*. *(14 points)*

______ **1.** Before the play begins, Walter Lee, Bobo, and Willy discuss buying a liquor store.

______ **2.** Mama slaps Beneatha for calling Walter a "flip."

______ **3.** George Murchison encourages the Youngers to take a greater interest in African history and culture.

______ **4.** Mama uses part of the money from Big Walter's insurance policy to buy a house in an all-white neighborhood.

______ **5.** The remainder of the money is lost when Willy swindles Walter.

______ **6.** Lindner returns to the Youngers' apartment because he wants to offer them more money not to move.

______ **7.** At the end of the play, Beneatha argues with Walter about her plans for the future.

Circle the letter of the best answer to each of the following items. *(16 points)*

8. A conflict takes place in Act One when

a. Walter Lee struggles to keep his job as a chauffeur.

b. Walter Lee struggles with other family members over money.

c. Travis struggles to keep up his grades in school.

d. Mama struggles with Ruth for control of the household.

9. Walter would like to see his family's life change in many ways. More than anything else, though, he wants to

a. buy Ruth nice things and live with her and Travis in a bigger house.

b. send Travis to a private school.

c. own a dry-cleaning business, like Charlie Atkins.

d. buy a liquor store with some friends.

10. Joseph Asagai does not give Beneatha

a. money for her medical training.

b. Nigerian records and clothing.

c. a Yoruba name.

d. a lecture on assimilationism.

11. In a private moment, Walter admits to Ruth that he

a. has been a disappointment to Big Walter and Lena.

b. wants to start looking for a new job.

c. doesn't know how to become close to her.

d. is afraid that he won't be able to support another child.

12. When Mama finally decides what to do with the insurance money, she

a. puts $3,500 down on a house and gives $6,500 to Walter to use as he wishes.

b. puts aside $3,500 for a European vacation, puts aside $3,500 for Beneatha's medical schooling, and gives the rest to Walter and Ruth.

c. puts aside $3,500 for a European vacation and asks Walter to decide how to spend the rest.

d. puts $3,500 down on a house, gives the rest to Walter to manage, and tells him to set aside $3,000 for Beneatha's medical schooling.

Name ______________________ Date ______________

TEST PART I: OBJECTIVE QUESTIONS *(cont.)*

13. As Lindner talks, the mood of Walter, Ruth, and Beneatha changes
- **a.** from tension to relief.
- **b.** from caution to interest to anger.
- **c.** from interest to surprise to confusion.
- **d.** from friendliness to fear.

14. Joseph Asagai's dream is to
- **a.** see Beneatha become a doctor someday.
- **b.** be a leader in Nigeria's fight for independence.
- **c.** open a school with Beneatha, in Nigeria.
- **d.** become a professor of political philosophy.

15. Mama decides to continue with the move to the house when
- **a.** she learns of Walter's plan to sell out to Lindner.
- **b.** she opens the present of gardening tools.
- **c.** she sees Travis cry at the thought of staying in the apartment.
- **d.** she finds out that Walter has managed to save some money.

Name ______________________________ Date ______________

TEST

PART II: SHORT-ANSWER QUESTIONS

Answer each question, using the lines provided. ***(40 points)***

16. Why does Mama not fully share her family's excitement about the check?

____

____

____

17. What is the difference between what George Murchison wants for Beneatha and what Joseph Asagai wants for her?

____

____

____

18. How would you describe the purpose of having Travis in this play?

____

____

____

19. Think about how the scene that opens Act Two inspires Walter and Beneatha to take pride in their heritage. How does that same kind of pride inspire both characters again near the end of the play?

____

____

____

20. What do Walter's thoughts about George Murchison suggest about his own personality?

____

____

____

Name ______________________ Date ______________

TEST

PART II: SHORT-ANSWER QUESTIONS *(cont.)*

21. How does the conversation with Mrs. Johnson illustrate the fact that Mama's purchase of a house has caused both joy and fear for her family?

____

____

____

22. Just before Lindner arrives, why does Walter say to Travis, "You just name it, son . . . and I hand you the world!"

____

____

____

23. Why is it ironic that Lindner refers to the topic of his discussion with the Youngers as one of Clybourne Park's "special community problems"?

____

____

____

24. Early in Act Three, Mama mourns, "Me and Big Walter just didn't never learn right." What does she mean? Does the end of the play prove her right—or wrong? Explain.

____

____

____

25. What major idea or ideas in the play does Mama's plant represent?

____

____

____

Name ______________________________ Date ______________

TEST PART III: ESSAY QUESTIONS

Choose two of the following topics. Use your own paper to write two or three paragraphs about each topic you choose. *(30 points)*

a. Walter Lee Younger clashes with other characters as the play progresses—that's **external conflict.** He also struggles with his own thoughts and feelings—that's **internal conflict.** Summarize Walter's external conflicts and internal conflicts in *A Raisin in the Sun.* Explain how both types of conflicts find some resolution by the end of the play.

b. According to Mama, Big Walter used to say, "Seem like God didn't see fit to give the black man nothing but dreams—but He did give us children to make them dreams seem worthwhile." Give specific details from the play to show how the **characters** of Walter and Beneatha make Mama (1) doubt her husband's words and (2) verify the truth of those words.

c. What is a **hero?** Think about heroic characters in books you have read, stories you have heard, or films or television programs you have seen. In your own words, explain what a hero is. Then identify someone from *A Raisin in the Sun* whom you would describe as a hero. Defend your choice by citing details from the play.

d. In his review of *A Raisin in the Sun* on its opening in 1959, critic Brooks Atkinson wrote that the play is "about human beings who want, on the one hand, to preserve their family pride and, on the other hand, to break out of the poverty that seems to be their fate." Think back over the play. Then explain, briefly, the point that *A Raisin in the Sun* makes about these major and minor **themes.**

- family pride
- escape from poverty
- humor
- the influence of environment on character
- pain

e. Plays often teach as well as entertain. How did reading *A Raisin in the Sun* help you understand the world at the time the events took place? How did it help you understand people and life today? List the details from the play that you found most helpful.

f. Discuss how one of the **Connections** that follow the play (HRW Library edition) is related to a theme, issue, or character in *A Raisin in the Sun.*

Use this space to make notes.

Answer Key

Act One

Making Meanings

READING CHECK

In Scene 1, our curiosity is aroused when Walter asks if the check is coming that day, and Ruth replies that it is due the next day and she doesn't want him to talk to her about it. Then Travis enters and mentions it. Later Walter talks about his plan to invest in a liquor store and urges Ruth to try and persuade Mama to consider it. Beneatha enters, and Walter talks about the cost of her education and about the check. Beneatha says, "The money belongs to Mama." Finally, we learn that the check is a payment on Mama's husband's life-insurance policy. The anticipation of the money is causing conflicts in the family.

Next Mama and Ruth discuss the money. Ruth promotes Walter's plan, and Mama declares that she will not help finance a liquor store because such a business goes against her convictions. We learn that the amount of the check is ten thousand dollars. Mama says that she will put part of it away for Beneatha's education and that she has been thinking of buying a house.

In Scene 2, Walter refers to the check when he talks to Willy Harris on the telephone. The whole family is eagerly awaiting its arrival. Later, Travis enters excitedly with an envelope, and Mama opens it. The conflict continues as Walter pleads to use the money to go into business.

1. Possible response: Walter's dream is being deferred; while Beneatha is studying to become a doctor, he is drying up "like a raisin in the sun."
2. Walter and Ruth argue about the time Travis spends in the bathroom, and about Walter's smoking in the morning. Ruth and Travis argue about the fifty cents Travis needs for a school project. Walter and Ruth argue about Walter's plan to invest in a liquor store. Beneatha and Walter argue about Beneatha's plan to go to medical school and about the insurance money.
3. Possible responses: Walter implies that Mama will listen more readily to Ruth than to Walter himself and that it is prudent to approach her indirectly. When Walter and Beneatha argue, Ruth advises them not to let Mama hear them.

   Mama enters with great dignity. Her bearing expresses nobility, and her features express strength. The stage directions suggest that she is heroic. Her voice is soft. In her first line she expresses concern about the "slamming doors," an indication that she is worried that her children have been arguing. In her next lines she shows her concern and love for Ruth: She tells her that she looks "peaked," and she offers to do some of the ironing. Later she reminds Beneatha to put on her robe because the room is drafty. When she sees Travis's messy bed, she excuses what she thinks are his attempts at tidiness. Finally, she expresses tenderness for her spindly houseplant.
4. Hansberry shows the strength of Mama's religious beliefs in the scene with Beneatha. When Beneatha claims she doesn't believe in the existence of God, Mama firmly reminds her that as long as she, Mama, is head of the family, Beneatha will acknowledge God. Perhaps most important, her faith is reflected in her refusal to contribute to the purchase of a liquor store because she doesn't want her involvement in a business she considers immoral on her "ledger." In all, the strength of her beliefs not only helps define Mama's character but also provides a cause for conflicts between her and her children, conflicts that may intensify as the play progresses.
5. Possible answer: As a Nigerian student in Chicago, Asagai represents a different, more international viewpoint. He is well traveled, liberal, and passionately convinced that the true roots and identity of African Americans are to be found in Africa. Asagai believes that African Americans should not yield to assimilation. Asagai stands in contrast to the goals and interests of George Murchison—the child of wealthy and successful African American par-

ents—which show that he has joined the mainstream of American society.

6. Some of the dramatic questions the playwright raises are: How will the insurance money be spent? What will Ruth do about her pregnancy? Will Beneatha marry Asagai or George Murchison? Will Mama keep the family together? Students' answers to their questions will vary.
7. Responses will vary. Students should include details from the play to support their opinions.
8. Sample response: Most adults would feel embarrassed, frustrated, or bitter about being lectured, spoken to as if they were children. Mama treats Walter like a child and holds him to a standard that may be unrealistic. All this makes Walter's dissatisfaction with his life more understandable.

■ Reading Strategies Worksheet

Organizing Information

(Responses will vary. Sample responses follow.)

Mama's Physical Appearance

1. She is "in her early sixties, full-bodied"; has dark-brown skin, white hair.
2. She has "unobtrusive" grace and beauty, a "noble bearing."
3. She has eyes that are "full of interest and expectancy."

Mama's Background

1. One of her children, Claude, died years earlier.
2. In the past she has provided for the family by doing "day work."
3. Her husband, Big Walter, died recently.

Mama's Interests and Concerns

1. She thinks a European vacation would be frivolous.
2. She demands that her children respect God in her home.
3. She admits that her children frighten her.

Mama's Actions

1. She slaps Beneatha for speaking disrespectfully about God.
2. She refuses to back Walter's plan to invest in a liquor store.
3. She condemns Walter for his attitude toward life and not showing support for Ruth's pregnancy.

Follow-up

- Mama's choices are linked to her values. Her respect for God and morality and her love for her family will affect her choices.
- Mama's refusal to back Walter's plan may be the most important action.

Act Two

■ Making Meanings

Reading Check

Scene 1: Beneatha and Walter celebrate their African heritage, but the excitement ends with the arrival of George Murchison, whom Walter ridicules. After George and Beneatha leave, Walter and Ruth talk with sadness about the state of their relationship. Mama returns with the news that she has bought a house in an all-white neighborhood.

Scene 2: The family has begun to pack for the move. A phone call from Walter's employer reveals that Walter has not been going to work. Walter describes the emptiness of his life. In response, Mama tells him that she has put $3,500 dollars down for the house but that he is to take charge of the remaining money, setting aside $3,000 for Beneatha's schooling. Made confident by Mama's trust, Walter promises Travis a good life in the years to come.

Scene 3: Walter's new assurance revives his marriage. Then, on moving day, the Youngers receive a visit from Karl Lindner, who brings a buyout offer. Walter, Ruth, and Beneatha refuse it. When Mama comes home, they joke to her about the offer and give her presents. The merriment is cut short, however, when Bobo brings the news that Willy has left town with all of the money for the liquor-store venture (including the money that Walter had failed to set aside for Beneatha's education).

1. Possible responses: Mama did the right thing in buying a house, but maybe she shouldn't have bought into such a troublesome neighborhood. Mama should not have given Walter the rest of the money; Walter already has expressed disapproval of Beneatha's desire to become a doctor and a willingness to break the law to speed up approval of a liquor license, and Mama is violating her conscience because she is fairly sure that he will invest in a liquor store. Mama did the right thing in giving Walter the money; for her, it is an apology for failing to treat Walter as an adult, and she thinks that her son will become a better person if she trusts him with the money.
2. In Greek mythology, Prometheus was a Titan, and Walter has spoken of himself as a giant. Prometheus brought fire to humanity; Walter has called himself a "volcano." Since Prometheus was punished horribly for his defiance of the gods, George implies that Walter's rantings are wrong-headed and that his dreams are fated to fail.
3. Answers will vary. The basic conflict between Walter and Ruth—the conflict that is the seed of their growing apart—is the result of Walter's materialistic ambition, which has almost completely overwhelmed his duties and his tenderness as a father and husband.
4. Beneatha's ambition to become a doctor is serious, and students may sympathize with her. It also is clear, however, that Beneatha is immature, allowing herself to become passionately involved in passing fancies (such as her photography lessons). In her eagerness to learn more about her African heritage, Beneatha's dressing in Nigerian costume and her rigidity in discussions with the rest of the family seem more than a bit comic. Overall, students generally will agree that the relatively complex and convincing characterization of Beneatha keeps her from becoming a mere stereotype.
5. She tells the news to Travis, her grandson. Her motivation appears to be linked with one of her major goals—her drive to preserve the stability and continuity of family life (seen, in part, in her promise that the house someday will be his).
6. Possible response: Lindner's tone is sympathetic, conciliatory, even apologetic. His message, however—no matter how positively presented—is one of prejudice and exclusion.
7. At the beginning of Scene 3, the mood is joyful and expectant; by the scene's end, all seems to have been lost. The first major reversal comes with Lindner's visit—from what appears to be a welcome to what turns out to be a proposal to keep the Youngers out of Clybourne Park. Mama's disturbance at news of Lindner's visit turns to pleasure and joy when the family gives her presents. This light moment, however, is shattered with Bobo's arrival and his news that the remaining money is gone.
8. Answers will vary. Encourage the students to support their responses with specific references to the play.
9. Sample answer: As a character contrasting with the Youngers, Mrs. Johnson points out their strengths—their emotional honesty, as opposed to her false enthusiasm; their quiet pride, as opposed to her gossip; their hope for the future, as opposed to her talk of the past. Her comments also foreshadow potential trouble should the Youngers move to Clybourne Park. Although Mrs. Johnson adds a touch of comic relief and does provide foreshadowing, Act Two could get along without her, especially given the threat associated with Lindner's visit in Scene 3.

Reading Strategies Worksheet

Drawing Conclusions

(Responses will vary. Sample responses follow.)

Mama ⟶ *Walter:* wants to see Walter act like a man

Walter ⟶ *Mama*: resents Mama's power (represented by her use of the money) but appreciates her more when she entrusts power to him

Mama → *Beneatha*: wants Beneatha to be happy, even if Mama doesn't always understand Beneatha's choices

Beneatha → *Mama*: appreciates Mama's understanding and courage and leans on her for emotional support when Bobo's news comes

Walter → *Beneatha*: somewhat resentful of Beneatha's chance for greater opportunities than he has had

Beneatha → *Walter*: sees that she and Walter are alike in some ways; probably angry at Walter when Bobo's news comes

Follow-up

- Mama decides to have Walter act as the head of the family and take responsibility for the family's future. In turn, Walter feels empowered and, with that empowerment, more encouraging of and kind to Mama—indeed, to everyone in the family. The revelation of the loss of the $6,500, however, implies that the relationship between Mama and Walter at the end of Act Two may be worse than it was at the end of Act One.
- Ruth is torn between the need to support Walter and the power of her own values, which are closer to Mama's. Travis probably does not understand much of the adults' feelings, but he probably is troubled to see so much arguing among them.

Act Three

■ Making Meanings

Reading Check

Walter stands up for his own dignity and that of his family. He puts aside material ambition to assert his essential humanity. The whole family is able to unite to preserve its basic dignity. In the face of that confrontation, the family's previous conflicts seem less significant.

1. Possible responses: The Youngers are heroic and brave; or they are in serious danger.
2. Asagai uses his own situation to show Beneatha the importance of not giving in to repressive circumstances, of taking action to improve one's lot. In essence, he is telling Beneatha that she need not abandon her dreams just because the insurance money is gone. His words also reaffirm themes of personal responsibility and of courage when times are difficult.
3. Possible answers: After Ruth has lived for years in the apartment, her nerves are almost ready to snap. She fears that if the family does not make a major change, neither she and Walter nor Travis will have a future.
4. Sample response: To get that money, he is willing to demean himself to an extent that Mama describes as being poorer than anyone in the family ever has been.
5. Possible answer: She warns Beneatha (who is several years younger than Walter and does not have his family responsibilities) not to judge a person until she considers the difficulties that the person has faced. She challenges Walter to break out of the kind of thinking and acting that he would be perpetuating if he accepted Lindner's offer—and to do it for the sake of his son.
6. Sample response: Our suspense is driven by the fear that Walter will sell out by making the deal with Lindner. Hansberry shows Walter frantically searching for a piece of paper, possibly the card with Lindner's telephone number; Walter then reveals his plan and bitterly parodies the actions of a defeated man begging a master for mercy. As he breaks down and retires to the bedroom, the audience is almost convinced that Walter is too unbalanced to heed Mama's words about human dignity. When the movers and Lindner arrive together, the suspense is intensified because of the need for an immediate decision—

and the suspense becomes even greater when Mama orders Travis to stay and listen to his father's words to Lindner.

7. Students may identify Mama and Walter as the most dynamic characters. Mama learns to understand Walter's torment, and she changes as she trusts and supports him more vigorously. Walter learns that he must stand up for his own dignity and must pay more attention to the needs of his wife and child. Students probably will agree that the play's minor characters—Travis, Asagai, George, Mrs. Johnson, Lindner, and Bobo—are static, but they may have varying views of Ruth and Beneatha.

8. Walter realizes the value of his own dignity and pride. Mama helps him make this realization possible; she also finds strength in her own love and support for her children.

9. Answer will vary. Possible responses: Things have gotten better in that more opportunities for education and employment are available to minorities today than when the play was written. Things have gotten worse in that racial tension continues. All parents and their adult children, regardless of race, still must figure out how to get along with each other, as must husbands and wives; dreams and goals continue to drive us; any dream postponed remains a source of frustration and conflict.

■ Reading Strategies Worksheet

Evaluating Cause and Effect

(Responses will vary. Sample responses follow.)

CAUSES

2. Asagai asks Beneatha to return to Nigeria with him, as his wife.

3. Ruth is desperate for the family to go through with the move.

6. Big Walter earned a house for the family through his hard work, which paid for the insurance policy.

7. Mama is proud of what her son has done.

EFFECTS

1. Beneatha decided that she wanted to become a doctor.

4. Mama tells Beneatha not to judge another person without measuring "what hills and valleys he come through."

5. Travis can then hear what Walter says to Lindner.

Follow-up: In *A Raisin in the Sun*, the "dream" relates primarily to the Youngers' desire to make a better life for themselves, starting with owning their home. Obstacles to that goal "defer" the dream. Statements 3 and 4 pit Ruth's desperation to own the house against Walter's desperation to get the money he wants to start a business, even if it means giving up the house. Statement 5 shows Beneatha's reaction to Walter's deferral of that dream (and her dream of medical school, as well). Statements 6 and 7 show the recapturing of that dream at the play's climax, and Statement 8 is Mama's reflection upon it.

Literary Elements Worksheets

■ Character and Characterization

(Responses will vary. Sample responses follow.)

WALTER LEE—AT THE BEGINNING

What he says: "You couldn't be on my side that long for nothing, could you?"

What other characters say about him: "You—you are a nut. Thee is mad, boy." (from Beneatha)

What the stage directions say about him: *in utter anguish as he brings his fists down on his thighs*

What he does: gives Travis money over Ruth's objections; challenges Beneatha's dream of becoming a doctor

WALTER LEE—AT THE END

What he says: "We have decided to move into our house because my father—my father—he earned it for us brick by brick."

What other characters say about him: "He finally come into his manhood today, didn't he?" (from Mama)

What the stage directions say about him: *The tension hangs; then WALTER steps back from it.*

What he does: puts his arms around Travis as he faces Lindner; urges the family to hurry their departure from the apartment

Follow-up: Answers will vary, depending upon the character chosen. For the characterization of Ruth Younger, for example, we have her own words of complaint about Mama's "meddling" (Act One, Scene 1), rejoicing over the prospect of a home of their own (Act Two, Scene 1), amusement over Beneatha's flightiness (Act One, Scene 1), and so on. Other characters' comments about her include Mama's concerns over Ruth's pregnancy (Act One, Scene 2) and Beneatha's support of Ruth's happiness about the move (Act Two, Scene 3). Stage directions that help characterize her are *affecting tea-party interest* (Act One, Scene 1) and *coming to him, gently and with misgiving, but coming to him* (Act Two, Scene 1). Characterizing actions include Ruth's singing of spirituals (Act One, Scene 1) and her purchase of used curtains for the new house (Act Two, Scene 3).

■ External and Internal Conflict

(Responses will vary. Sample responses follow.)

1. Walter wants Mama to underwrite his plan to invest in a liquor store; Mama does not want to see him involved in such a business.
2. Mama would like to solve Walter's problems for him, but she knows that he needs to take responsibility for solving problems on his own.
3. When Ruth expresses concern for the family and especially for Travis, Walter feels that she is rejecting the big dreams that would support him.
4. Although Walter knows that he is not the husband and father that he should be, he is driven by the desire to have the lifestyle of the people he envies.
5. The Youngers are willing to prove that they will be good neighbors; Lindner speaks on behalf of people who are unwilling to give them the chance.

Follow-up

- Walter wants to see Beneatha take on more traditional dreams and do more to support the family; Beneatha wants to blaze her own trail. Ruth wants to be supportive of her husband, but she disagrees with some of his ideas.
- Seeing some of the Youngers' internal conflicts helps us understand these people and their external conflicts better. Internal conflicts also show that they are round characters, not mere two-dimensional figures.

■ Motivation

(Responses will vary. Sample responses follow.)

1. *MAMA*
   MOTIVATIONS: has worked hard all her life without getting ahead; worries about her children and grandchild
   ACTION: buys a house in hopes of giving the family a better life and a brighter future
2. *WALTER LEE*
   MOTIVATIONS: envies what richer people have; tired of working for others instead of being his own boss
   ACTION: violates Mama's trust by investing—and losing—$6,500 in the liquor-store venture
3. *ASAGAI*
   MOTIVATIONS: desperate for his people's improvement; willing to take risks
   ACTION: plans to return to Africa, even if he is murdered as a result of his work there
4. *LINDNER*
   MOTIVATIONS: unwilling to see anyone get hurt; knows that the Clybourne Park Improvement Association will hold him accountable
   ACTION: revisits the Youngers with a buyout offer

Follow-up

- Walter Lee's motives are primarily self-serving. It is no surprise that he comes into conflict with Mama (who, he thinks, is trying to deny him his chance for success) and Beneatha (who, he thinks, wants to see her dreams fulfilled at the expense of his own).
- Students may choose Mama, whose motivations focus on seeing the good in others or wanting good things to happen for them, or Asagai, whose motivations focus on his love and hopes for his nation.

Vocabulary Worksheet

If you wish to score this worksheet, assign the point values given in parentheses.

A. *(4 points each)*

1. c **7.** c
2. a **8.** d
3. a **9.** a
4. b **10.** d
5. d **11.** c
6. b **12.** b

B. *(4 points each)*

13. permeated
14. exasperated
15. furtively
16. revelation
17. agitated

C. *(4 points each)*

18. h **22.** b
19. e **23.** c
20. f **24.** a
21. d **25.** g

Exploring the Connections

A Letter from the Playwright

Reading Check

a. Hansberry is writing to her mother, shortly before *A Raisin in the Sun* opens in New Haven, Connecticut.

b. The play is supposed to show that African Americans "are just as complicated" as white people are—just as capable of knowing misery and just as capable of acting with dignity.

1. She wants the cast members to be proud of their participation and go on to long, satisfying careers as actors; she also wants investors in the play to be pleased with the play's financial as well as artistic success.

2. She wants white people to stop viewing African Americans as simple folk or people who do not understand the concept of human dignity.

3. Choices will vary; the "truths" may relate to common qualities in all people, some aspect of human relationships, and more.

Connecting with the Play

Many students will suggest that Mama has the most dignity, for she has shown herself strong in a lifetime marked by hard times and is trying to share that strength with her children. Walter recaptures his dignity in his final meeting with Lindner, so he is another choice. Other choices are possible but should be defended with details from the play.

Chicago: Southside Summers

Reading Check

a. The Hansberrys were never to betray their family and never to betray their race.

b. She is surprised to think that her father, despite his accomplishments, "must have known *fear*."

c. She wants to use her father's example to protest something that the newspaper has said about the civil rights movement.

1. Hansberry characterizes her parents as efficient and as expecting their children to meet high standards but also as undemonstrative with their love. Her siblings were likewise undemonstrative; and although they may have helped take care of her, they considered her a nuisance and tried to avoid her.
2. The images are vivid—young Hansberry's being abused on the way to and from school and her mother's guarding their house, gun in hand. The images help show that the problems faced by African Americans are very real—and much in need of solution, as she points out repeatedly.
3. Answers will be personal and need not be shared. In general, students who want to tell their stories honestly probably would present an image with both positive and negative characteristics.
4. Some students may feel that the fragmentation created by this approach is distracting, but many students may suggest that the approach underscores the fact that a person's life and personality are complex and rich.

Connecting with the Play

Students may cite Walter Lee's explosive temper and the upheavals that he creates in the lives of other family members as he complains of his dissatisfactions and as he takes risks with the family's future.

■ My Dungeon Shook

Reading Check

a. Baldwin is writing on the centennial of the freeing of all enslaved African Americans.

b. According to Baldwin, *integration* occurs when African Americans force white Americans "to see themselves as they are" and thus to change the false reality that has been an obstacle to race relations.

1. Questions may include why he feels that Charles Dickens's writings describe the lives of modern African Americans, how he might try to get white Americans to understand his definition of *integration*, what role he wants his nephew to take in the civil rights movement, and so on.
2. Baldwin feels that his "country" and "countrymen" have committed the past and present crime of destroying "hundreds of thousands of lives" through prejudice.
3. Students may suggest that the subject matter is difficult and that perhaps Baldwin kept thinking of changes that might express his ideas to a young teenager more effectively.

Connecting with the Play

In general, Baldwin seems to have faith that young people can do much to change the world. In particular, when he describes James's birth, he points out that though the boy's parents "had every reason to be heavyhearted, yet they were not," because love for him gave them the strength to survive.

■ Home

Reading Check

a. The family is having trouble meeting mortgage payments on the house, and Papa has gone to the lenders to ask for another extension. If he fails, the family will lose the house.

b. The women sit on the porch and talk, mostly about the importance of the house and how they will cope if they have to leave it.

1. Students who appreciate a "happy ending" may have expected Papa to return with good news, especially because the story is so short that a further complication seems unlikely. Students who were surprised may have been led by events in *A Raisin in the Sun* to expect that Papa would meet with some sort of prejudice that would complicate the problem.
2. The overall mood is tense, with a suspense that builds dramatically as Brooks describes in great detail the sight of Papa walking toward the house with news that the family is waiting to hear.

3. Helen pretended that the house was not pretty and that she would not want to have some of her friends see it, but the story concludes with her thinking about giving a party so that her friends can see the house. Her pretense underscores the importance of this home, in particular, and the importance of a home to one's family.

Connecting with the Play

Some students will feel that *Home* is an appropriate title because (1) the Youngers feel that a home of their own will improve all their lives and (2) the play explores the conflicts within their present home. Other students may prefer the current title because of its reference to the dreams that each of the Youngers cherishes.

■ 2239 North 16th Street

Reading Check

a. Unlike the neighboring houses, 2239 North 16th Street is inhabited only by women.

b. Bebe's mother believes that an integrated school will give Bebe a better education (a "white" education) and thus a better chance for future success.

c. While upset, Bebe threatens to take a knife to Miss Bradley "if she messes with me."

1. Possible response: Jennie G.'s words to Miss Bradley are the first time we see that Bebe herself is the target of prejudice. The information makes us rethink everything else in the story. It refocuses the narrative from a humorous personal memoir to a statement about racism.

2. The women want "Achievement!" from her; she is "to *do* something" with her life, whether she likes it or not. Similarly, Miss Bradley sets high standards for her students and expects everyone in class to rise to the challenge.

3. What sets Bebe off is hearing Sandra say, "My father made me a beautiful dollhouse for my birthday." This may be a statement of fact or just a made-up sentence to illustrate a spelling word, but it seems to make Bebe realize and resent the fact that other children have things (a dollhouse, a father at home) that she does not.

Connecting with the Play

Jennie G.'s expectation of certain behavior from African Americans reflects the prejudice that has made the Youngers' lives so hard. Specifically, it is this prejudice that makes the residents of Clybourne Park eager to stop the Youngers from moving into their community. Students may suggest that none of the characters in the play resembles Jennie G. (for even Lindner seems somewhat sympathetic to the Youngers' situation) but that unseen characters—Mr. Arnold, for example, or members of the Clybourne Park Improvement Association—may be like her.

■ Everything That Rises Must Converge

Reading Check

a. At her insistence, he is accompanying her downtown to "a reducing class at the Y."

b. She feels that African Americans had better lives when they were enslaved and that if they must "rise," they should stay "on their own side of the fence." She does not want to mix with them in her daily activities.

c. Carver's mother shouts and hits Julian's mother with her handbag hard enough to knock her senseless, perhaps seriously so.

1. Answers will vary; students may suggest that Julian's mother should learn some sort of lesson but that what happens to her is too serious to be deserved. (Indeed, if she recovers, she may think that the attack reinforces her view.)

2. Possible response: Julian is angry at himself. He seems to have no future (nor any strong desire for one), and he resents the fact that the aspects of his heritage that appeal to him are unavailable to him. Perhaps he finds it more convenient to blame his mother—rightly or wrongly—and spend his life in a bitter sulk than to take action and improve matters. His mother is and always has been rather innocent, and her frequent lack of reaction to his venom may be a part of her innocence. She truly seems to love him, as well, and thus may want to believe the best about him.

3. Julian fantasizes about the things he might do to upset his mother and about the house he would like to have. Furthermore, his belief that he "was not dominated by his mother" seems a fantasy, for he is at her beck and call (albeit resentfully) throughout the story.

4. Answers will vary and may be based upon students' thoughts about the mother's possible recovery. O'Connor's story, however, ends with the implication that what happens to Julian's mother will cause Julian to be overwhelmed by "the world of guilt and sorrow."

Connecting with the Play

Like the Youngers, Julian wants to get away from the neighborhood in which he now is living in order to have a better life. His dream, however, is to have "a place where the nearest neighbors would be three miles away on either side."

■ The March to Montgomery

Reading Check

a. Voting rights were important because in many places in the South, African Americans were barred from voting or registering to vote.

b. In the chaos at the march on the first day, he was hit on the head, probably by a policeman's nightstick.

c. The "second phase" of the march included people from all walks of life, marching together.

d. The military, under the direction of President Johnson, protected marchers, making it possible for them to assemble and express their frustration for the entire world to see.

1. Answers will vary; most students will point out that Lewis's vivid descriptions give the piece a great deal of emotional force and pull readers into the suspense of the march. Responses should also allude to at least one of these descriptions: the bodies trampled by horses, the concussion that Lewis sustains, or the image of people from all walks of life marching together.

2. Tragically, the Rev. James Reeb, a white minister who supported the march, was beaten by a group of white men in Selma. At this point, President Johnson responded, with a televised speech and a call to the military to protect the marchers. Ironically, it took the death of a white man to turn the march into the unqualified success that it became.

3. Possible response: As a symbolic event, the march made a lasting impression worldwide. People will always remember Martin Luther King, Jr.'s bravery and wisdom. More tangibly, the march changed history by making it easier for African Americans to voice their political concerns through voting.

Connecting with the Play

The Youngers are obviously interested in civil rights, as their brave decision to integrate a white neighborhood demonstrates. However, they seem to be alone in their quest. Their neighbors do not necessarily support or understand their decision. By 1965 the civil-rights movement had gained enough force that the Youngers might have felt their decision was part of a movement and not the brave resolve of an isolated family.

Test

■ Part I: Objective Questions

1. T	**6.** F	**11.** c
2. F	**7.** T	**12.** d
3. F	**8.** b	**13.** b
4. T	**9.** d	**14.** b
5. T	**10.** a	**15.** a

Part II: Short-Answer Questions

Answers may vary; possible answers are given.

16. Mama still grieves for Big Walter, who meant more to her than any insurance check. Mama also may sense the approach of conflicts over the use of the money, especially given Walter's general dissatisfaction with his life.

17. George Murchison wants Beneatha to look good for him (and thus to make him look good) but not to try to change him in any way. Joseph Asagai wants Beneatha to become all that she can be; in particular, he wants her to "live the answer" to the problems that seem to stand in the way of her dreams, as he does with his own problems.

18. Being a child, Travis represents the future, and all of the Youngers dream of a better "tomorrow." Furthermore, the difference in the ways that his parents treat him underscores the conflicts that they have with each other.

19. Walter talks about the family's pride in its members and tells Lindner that Travis is the sixth generation of the family in the United States (a reminder that the family's origins are in Africa). He then turns down the buyout offer out of faithfulness to the memory of his father, who earned the house for them "brick by brick." Walter's pride in his heritage makes him "come into his manhood" at this pivotal moment. Inspired by Walter's example, Beneatha also recaptures her dream of helping others. She ends the play with a revised dream—of taking the skills that she will learn back to Africa, the land of their heritage.

20. Walter is jealous and insecure. George's money, fine clothes, and education remind Walter that he struggles financially, must do without, and works at an unskilled job in which he must serve someone else.

21. Mrs. Johnson begins by emoting over the fact that the Youngers are about to "move on up a little higher"—a rather apt summary of what the Youngers hope to achieve in their new home. Quickly, however, she goes on to talk about the violence that African Americans are facing in all-white communities and imagines reading that the Youngers' house in Clybourne Park has been bombed. This talk recaptures the worry that Mama's children already have expressed about living in an all-white area.

22. Mama has just entrusted Walter with the balance of the insurance money and has urged him to be the head of the family. Filled with new self-esteem and a sense of the potential for success that the money represents, Walter feels that he can promise his son a great future.

23. The irony of Lindner's words lies in the fact that in the eyes of the Clybourne Park Improvement Association, the Youngers are the problem. Lindner is seeking their help in solving the problem, but his solution is that they not be part of the community.

24. Mama is remembering that when she was younger, she was warned about setting her goals too high. Like Big Walter, she dared to have big dreams. At this point in the play, those dreams have come crashing down, and Mama regrets that she and her husband didn't listen to the warnings, years earlier. Mama is proven wrong at the end of the play, for her children—Walter, especially—do reclaim a big dream for themselves and the family.

25. The plant represents the importance of enduring: As Mama manages to keep it alive, despite less-than-ideal conditions, the Youngers manage to stay together as a family and see some of their dreams begin to come true. The plant also represents growth, and several of the characters in the play—especially Walter, Mama, and perhaps Beneatha—mature as they work through their problems.

PART III: Essay Questions

a. Responses will vary. Students should note that Walter has external conflicts with every other major character in the play, as well as with most of the minor characters. He clashes with Mama over their differing opinions about what is important in life; he clashes with Ruth over their parenting of Travis and their own fragile relationship; he clashes with Beneatha over her desire to become a doctor. He clashes with all three over the use of the insurance money. His internal conflicts arise from clashes among his desire to get the money that he thinks will give him and his family a better future, his need (rarely acknowledged) to be a better husband and father, and his pride in himself and his heritage. At the end of the play—specifically, when he clashes with Lindner by turning down the sellout offer—he regains the respect of his family and his own self-respect.

b. Students may point out that when Walter, abusing the trust that Mama has placed in him, loses his and Beneatha's portion of the insurance money to Willy Harris, he gives Mama reason to doubt that children are an encouragement to dreams. To a lesser extent, Beneatha's loss of faith in her own dream of becoming a doctor (since Walter has lost the money that would fund her training) seems to deny the value of Big Walter's words. When Walter and Beneatha regain their dreams through the refusal of the offer from the Clybourne Park Improvement Association, however, their father's words seem more true and glorious than ever.

c. Students are likely to include physical or intellectual achievements or—especially—acts of courage in their definitions of the term *hero*. They probably will identify Mama as a hero for trying to keep her family together or Walter as a hero for ultimately standing up for himself, his family, and his heritage in the face of prejudice. To a lesser extent, Joseph Asagai and Beneatha also display heroic qualities in wanting to improve the lives of the people around them.

d. Explanations may resemble the following:

- family pride: pride in a family's heritage and present generation can provide support when problems arise; family problems can spin out of control when family members are driven by wrongful pride.
- escape from poverty: it takes great courage to escape poverty; the chance to escape poverty may force people to reassess their values.
- humor: if you look for it, you can find humorous moments throughout the day; humor can defuse a tense situation.
- pain: we would get along better if we understood each other's private pain; sometimes the people who should give you the greatest joy cause the deepest pain.
- the influence of environment on character: people who have to "do without" for a long time may act out of character to change their situation; if a person lives in an environment where dreams are lovingly encouraged, that person will help make dreams come true.

e. Students may suggest that *A Raisin in the Sun* shed light on a historical period that they knew only from classroom study; that it helped them see how similar people are, despite differences of generation, location, or race; and that it reminded them that the support of one's family can help a person deal with the challenges in his or her life. Details will vary but may draw upon various exchanges of dialogue or the topic of prejudice, which shapes almost every aspect of the play.

f. Responses will vary according to class interaction with the **Connections** selections.

Notes

Notes

Notes

Notes

Notes

Notes

Notes

Notes

Notes